COMP

BR LS

for less™

includes
DISCOUNT COUPONS FOR ATTRACTIONS & MUSEUMS

the guidebook that pays for itself in one day

Brussels for less

Compact Guide

Publisher Information

First published in Great Britain in 1999 by Metropolis International (UK) Ltd.

ISBN 1 901811 01 8

COPYRIGHT

DISCLAIMER

Assessments of attractions, hotels, museums and so forth are based on the author's impressions and therefore contain an element of subjective opinion that may not reflect the opinion of the publishers.

The contents of this publication are believed to be correct at the time of printing. However, details such as opening times will change over time. We would advise you to call ahead to confirm important information.

All organizations offering discounts in this guidebook have a contract with the publisher to give genuine discounts to holders of valid *for less* vouchers.

The publisher and/or its agents will not be responsible if any establishment breaches its contract (although it will attempt to secure compliance) or if any establishment changes ownership and the new owners refuse to honour the contract.

Care has been taken to ensure that discounts are only offered at reputable establishments, however, the publisher and/or its agents cannot accept responsibility for the quality of merchandise or service provided, nor for errors or inaccuracies in this guidebook.

The publisher will not be held responsible for any loss, damage, injury, expense or inconvenience sustained by any person, howsoever caused, as a result of information or advice contained in this guide except insofar as the law prevents the exclusion of such liability.

PUBLISHER

Metropolis International
222 Kensal Road
London W10 5BN
England

Telephone:
+44-(0)181-964-4242
(After May 2000, tel:
+44-(0)20-8964-4242)

Fax:
+44-(0)181-964-4141
(After May 2000, fax:
+44-(0)20-8964-4141)

E-mail:
admin@for-less.com

Web site:
http://www.for-less.com

ABBREVIATIONS

- ☎ Telephone Number
- Ⓜ Nearest metro station
- 🕒 Opening times

Contents

HOW TO OBTAIN DISCOUNTS

Many of the museums and attractions in this guide offer discounts to holders of this book.

Museums and attractions which offer a discount are highlighted in pink in the text and designated by the following symbol in the margins:

for less

To obtain your discount, simply hand in the appropriate voucher from the back of the book when you purchase your ticket.

Introduction to Brussels

Atomium

Brussels likes to call itself the heart of Europe and it has some powerful evidence to back up this claim. It is the home of the Council of Ministers, where many of the decisions of European politics are made. It also houses the European Commission, the EU's executive arm, and the headquarters of NATO.

Whatever your views on the European Union, you will not want to get bogged down with the intricacies of politics when you are on holiday. Brussels also offers a feast of culture, drama, heritage and gastronomy for tourists.

History is all around you here in the elegant facades of buildings, many of which date back to the Middle Ages, and in the winding streets of the central area.

The guild houses in the **Grand Place** (page 10), which are a good starting point from which to explore the old centre, are wonderful examples of 17th-century architecture. They are also reminders that Brussels was once the centre of Europe's lace and tapestry-making industries.

Near the Grand Place is arguably Brussels' most famous monument, the statue of a small boy urinating into a fountain.

Did You Know ...?

Brussels has a population of 1 million, a quarter of which is made up of people not of Belgian descent.

Affectionately known as the **Manneken Pis** (page 11), it is one of the most photographed statues in Europe, and is dressed in costume on certain days of the year.

Brussels' medieval city centre extends around the Grand Place and is a manageable size for exploration on foot. It is enclosed within boulevards which follow the path of the 14th-century city walls, which now no longer exist.

The centre is subdivided into quarters, each with their own specific identities. In addition to the elegant area of commerce around the Grand Place, there is the picturesque **Le Sablon** district in the south and the winding streets of **Ste-Catherine** to the west, centred around the 14th-century church of the same name.

The **Ilot Sacré** area is a particular favourite with tourists, with its clusters of medieval streets named after food types and its numerous excellent restaurants.

For respite on a warm day, head for the **Parc de Bruxelles** in the east, or for shelter on a rainy day, visit one of the major museums surrounding it – the **Musée d'Art Moderne** (page 22), the **Musée d'Art Ancien** (page 21) and the **Musée de la Dynastie** (page 19) are all nearby.

Other excellent museums in the city

Grand Place

centre include the **Musée de la Ville de Bruxelles** (page 11) in the Grand Place, the **Centre Belge de la Bande Dessinée** (page 15), devoted to the history of the comic strip, and the excellent **Musée du Cinéma** (page 20).

Outside the centre, the north of the city is the location of attractions such as **Mini Europe** (page 28) and the **Atomium** (page 27), as well as the 19th-century **Château Royal** (page 27) and the church of **Notre Dame de Laeken** (page 26).

Don't Miss

The Serres Royales (page 27), lovely greenhouses housing tropical and temperate plants in the Domaine Royal de Laeken.

The **Parc du Cinquantenaire** area, east of the city centre, is another important stopping point – it is home to the **Musées Royaux** (pages 30, 33 and 35), which cover arts, sciences and military history.

Although it is located in the southern, French-speaking, part of the country, Brussels' position as the capital city means that Belgium's two languages have equal status here. All the streets have two names – one in French, the other in Flemish. Visitors will, however, find that most people in Brussels speak English.

Parc de Cinquantenaire

The legacy of Belgium's history as a colonial power can be seen in the immigrant, and now second generation, populations of people from central Africa, notably Zaire which was once the Belgian Congo. More recently, Brussels' reputation as the capital of Europe is furthering the city's claim to be a cultural crossroads.

One of the great joys of Brussels is eating and drinking. The restaurants are superb, if a little expensive, and often serve local specialities as well as national and international cuisine.

The choice of beers is nothing short of incredible. Forget the brand names you know back home – here there are hundreds of different ones to choose from, all in uniquely shaped glasses and carrying their own specially designed labels.

The bar staff in most places will be glad to help you understand the list of beers that you will be given on entering a bar. They will suggest which are the lighter ones and which are the heavier ones that might cause you problems getting to your feet at the end of the evening. Many people order some paté and smoked cheese with crackers to go with the beer, even if they have already eaten.

IF YOU DO ONE THING . . .

1. If you visit one museum . . . the **Musée du Cinéma** (page 20)
2. If you visit one church . . . **St. Michel et Ste. Gudule** (page 17)
3. If you go to one attraction . . . **Mini Europe** (page 28)
4. If you go to one theatre . . . the **Théâtre de la Monnaie** (page 53)
5. If you walk in one park . . . **Parc du Cinquantenaire** (page 32)
6. If you dine in one restaurant . . **Toone VII** (page 50)
7. If you go to one art gallery . . . the **Musée d'Art Moderne** (page 22)
8. If you go shopping . . . **Galeries St. Hubert** (page 13)
9. If you go on one excursion . . . **Bruges** (page 42)
10. If you stroll in one square . . . **Grand Place** (page 10)

Being the centre of Europe, Brussels has a fast and efficient communications network to other northern European capitals and throughout the rest of Belgium. Trains to **Bruges** (page 42) and **Ostend** (page 49) take roughly an hour, to **Antwerp** (page 47) or **Ghent** (page 48) half that time, which means day trips from Brussels are easy and cheap to take.

Paris is just a few hours away on the mainline express route frequented by Euro politicians. The two-hour train ride to Luxembourg will take you through the magnificent forests of the Ardennes in southern Belgium and then through northern Luxembourg, past fairytale castles clinging to their mountain tops.

History of Brussels

Archaeologists have proved there was a **Neolithic** settlement on the site of Brussels long before it became part of the **Roman Empire** in 15 BC. The area remained marshy and largely uninhabited until the 7th century, when the settlement became known as **Bruocsella**, "the village in the marshes".

Over the years merchants and craftsmen came here and erected a fortified dwelling. Later the **Counts of Louvain** took control of the settlement and put up extra defences. The city grew in political and commercial strength and a second wall was erected in 1379 along the line of the current inner ring-road.

Reflections

'I'm not Caucasian, I'm Belgian' – Toots Thielemans, Belgian jazz musician

In the 15th century the reign of the **Louvains** came to an end with the death of the **Duchess Jeanne**, and the **House of Burgundy** took control of the city, using it as the location of their court. The presence of the Dukes of Burgundy in the town ensured that the 15th century was a period of economic growth.

In 1494, rule over Brussels and the surrounding area passed to Charles V, who later became king of Spain and Holy Roman Emperor. On Charles V's abdication in 1555, his son **Philip II** succeeded as king of Spain and of the Low Countries (today's Belgium, Luxembourg and the Netherlands).

Fanatically Catholic, Philip introduced the **Spanish Inquisition** to his territories. This was partly responsible for the revolt of the seven northern provinces and the formation of the **Independent United Provinces** which became the Netherlands. A similar revolt in Brussels and the southern territories was put down, and the city became part of the Spanish Netherlands.

In the 17th century, Spanish power was so weakened that they were unable to defend their territory, and Brussels was caught up in a series of wars. In 1713 the **Treaty of Utrecht** gave the Spanish Netherlands to the **Austrian emperors**, who allowed their subjects greater autonomy.

Much of the elegant architecture that is obvious today is thanks to the foresight of **Charles of Lorraine** who governed the city from 1744. Notably, there were renovations to the **Place Royale** and the church of **St. Jacques sur Coudenberg**.

With the **French Revolution** in full flood just a few miles to the west, 1789 also saw the start of the **Brabant Uprising** against Austria, which was suppressed. From 1795 until 1815, when **Napoleon** was defeated at Waterloo, the territory was annexed to France. At the **Treaty of Vienna**, Brussels was made joint capital of the new united Netherlands.

Following an explosive performance at the **Théâtre de la Monnaie** (Opera House) in 1830, the people of Brussels sparked off the Revolution that was to lead to independence for their country. **Leopold Saxe-Coburg** was crowned the first King of the Belgians the following year.

Then began a period of rapid growth which saw Brussels develop into a modern, world-class city. The arts and education flourished, buildings and roads were constructed, transport and communications were modernised. In 1880 the city staged the **International Exhibition** to mark 50 years of independence.

The **First** and **Second World Wars** took their toll on Belgium in terms of lives lost and buildings destroyed, but the country pulled itself up again after each conflict and in 1959 it was designated as the headquarters of the **European Commission**. Eight years later **NATO** established its HQ here too. Since then the city has gone from strength to strength and now plays host to diplomats from all over the European Union and hundreds of thousands of tourists each year.

Maison du Roi

Central Brussels

Grand Place

Walking into the **Grand Place** (or Grote Markt in Flemish) for the first time is a marvellous experience. Its handsome facades, flying flags and flower beds have a picture-postcard prettiness. The formal style of the square also gives it a sense of authority and architectural elegance.

The Grand Place was the centre of commerce and so became the site for guildhouses, the offices of the city's trade associations. They are still identifiable today as each one adopted a symbol and a nickname. The Archers' Guild, for instance, chose the she-wolf as their symbol, while the Bakers picked Charles II of Spain.

The Grand Place can get crowded, especially in the summer months, but it is easy to escape down one of the adjoining streets or into a café.

Taking centre stage is the **Hôtel de Ville** (Town Hall) whose hefty tower rises from one flank of the building. The facade has recently been cleaned and it is now sparkling. Parts date back to the first years of the 15th century, others (including the tower) to the mid-1400s, although it was heavily restored about 100 years ago.

On closer inspection you will see that the facade is lined with statues, again dating from the 15th century. Many are well

Grand Place

Ⓜ Gare Centrale

Hôtel de Ville

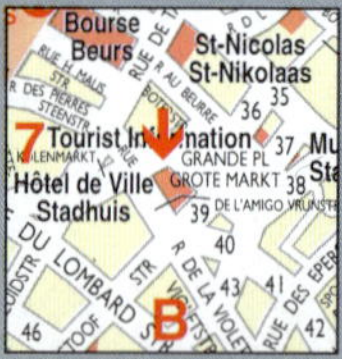

Grand Place
Ⓜ Gare Centrale
☎ 513 8940
Call for times of guided tours.
Admission charge.

preserved considering the beating they must have taken from the weather over nearly 600 winters.

It is possible to take a walking tour through the Town Hall and see the impressive wall-hangings and tapestries in the main Council Chamber. There are breathtaking views from the tower, which is accessible as part of the tour.

The **Musée de la Ville de Bruxelles** (Municipal Museum) is situated in the Maison du Roi (King's House) which is the central building opposite the Town Hall across the Grand Place. The building dates from the 16th century but has suffered extensive damage so most of what you see today is more recent.

The museum has been open for more than 100 years and shows collections pertaining to the history of Brussels and its local arts and crafts.

There are some remarkably detailed tapestries on display. Look out, too, for the paintings, altarpieces, sculptures and ceramics. There is also a display showing how Brussels has developed over the years, and the history of the city is illustrated by maps, models and photographs. The museum also displays the wardrobe of the Manneken Pis.

Musée de la Ville de Bruxelles

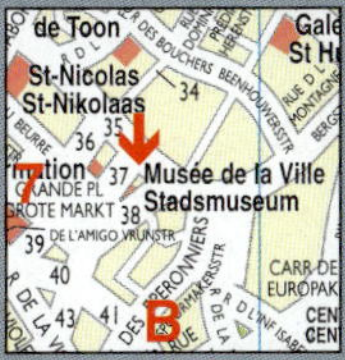

Maison du Roi, Grand Place
Ⓜ Gare Centrale
☎ 511 27 42
🕒 May-Sep: Mon-Fri: 10am-12.30pm, 1.30pm-5pm. Sat & Sun: 10am-1pm. Oct-Apr: Mon-Fri: 10am-12.30pm, 1.30pm-4pm.
Admission charge.
2 admissions for the price of 1 with voucher on page 67.

It is quite hard to find the **Manneken Pis**, which seems strange as it must rank as one of the world's most famous eccentric monuments. It is on a street corner behind railings and is invariably surrounded by people snapping away with cameras. The statue is of a

Hôtel de Ville

Musée du Costume et de la Dentelle

small boy answering the call of nature which was designed, bizarrely, as a drinking fountain by Jerome Duquesnoy the Elder in 1619.

The poor little lad has had a turbulent history. He has been stolen many times, nearly always, it seems, by drunken soldiers as a trophy of their night on the town. At different times of the year he is dressed in appropriate costumes from the wardrobe at the Musée de la Ville de Bruxelles. He becomes an RAF pilot on September 15 to commemorate the Battle of Britain and a US sailor on October 27 to celebrate Navy Day.

Manneken Pis

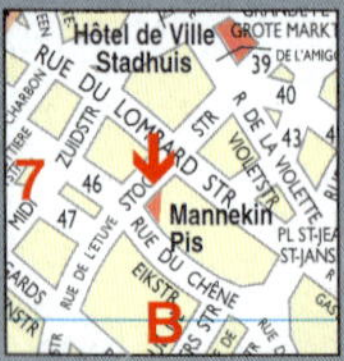

Corner of Rue de l'Etuve and Rue du Chene
Ⓜ Bourse

So expert were the Brussels lacemakers that the city became famous for producing some of the world's finest lace cloth and adornments. Traders from far and wide were commissioned to seek it out and take back samples for the nobility. The **Musée du Costume et de la Dentelle** (Costume and Lace Museum) traces the history of this brand of fashion back over the centuries and shows how Brussels succeeded in cornering much of the world's lace market.

There are some exquisite examples of ancient and modern lacework which were always the preserve of the rich. It is no wonder such items were so expensive when you consider the amount of effort the laceworkers went to in order to produce even the smallest pieces.

The **Eglise St. Nicholas** (Church of St. Nicholas) is Brussels' oldest church. It was begun in the 12th century and has gone through various periods of destruction and rebuilding to reach the state visitors see it in today.

It was originally built near an old stream, a geographical problem which forced the stone masons to construct a chapel at an odd angle so as not to build over the water. The church is a treasure trove of ecclesiastical works of art and ornaments and is well worth a short visit.

The **Théâtre de Toone** (Puppet Theatre) stages unique performances. Here classic works are performed not by actors but puppets in full costume. The puppeteers are masters of illusion. *(6 impasse Schuddeveld, Petite rue des Bouchers, Ⓜ Bourse, ☎ 511 7137. ⏲ Tue-Sat: 12noon-12midnight.)*

L'Ilot Sacré is a cluster of medieval streets to the east of the Grand Place. Stallholders have sold their tantalising wares here since the Middle Ages, and it is still one of the liveliest areas in Brussels for restaurants and grocery shopping.

The **Galeries St. Hubert** opened in 1846 with the proud boast that it was the first glass-ceilinged shopping arcade in Europe, possibly the world. Since then many countries have copied its design. The elegance of the arcade is reflected not only in the architecture but in the choice of shops and the price tags of their goods.

Musée du Costume et de la Dentelle

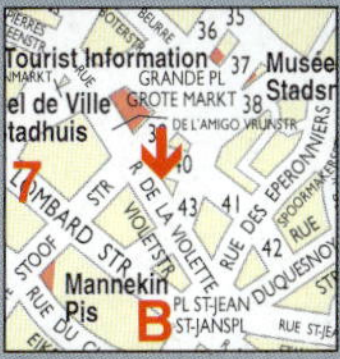

Rue de la Violette
Ⓜ Bourse
☎ 512 77 09
⏲ Apr-Sep: Mon, Tue, Thu, Fri: 10am-12.30pm, 1.30pm-5pm. Sat & Sun 2pm-5.30pm. Oct-Mar: Mon, Tue, Thu, Fri: 10am-12.30pm, 1.30pm-4pm. Sat & Sun: 2pm-4pm.
Admission charge.
2 admissions for the price of 1 with voucher on page 67.

Eglise St. Nicholas

Rue au Buerre
Ⓜ Bourse
☎ 513 80 22
⏲ Mon-Sun: 7.45am-6.30pm.

Manneken Pis

Galeries St. Hubert

Here you will find stores selling delicate lace, fine shoes and the most delicious chocolates. There are also some cafés where you can recover from spending too much money.

Galeries St. Hubert

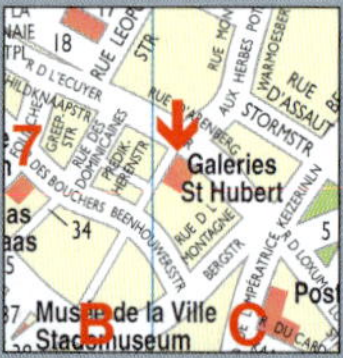

Ⓜ Gare Centrale

The **Théâtre de la Monnaie** (Opera House) is regarded as one of the world's leading opera houses. It regularly hosts spectacular performances and international premieres. Visitors usually get only as far as the elegant, columned facade, for tickets are extremely popular and hard to buy. Call ahead for availability and go along on the night to check for returned tickets.

The opera house gained notoriety in 1830 when an inflammatory opera sparked first the audience and then much of the city into revolution that led to Belgium becoming an independent country for the first time.

Théâtre de la Monnaie

Place de la Monnaie, Rue Leopold
Ⓜ De Brouckère
☎ 229 12 11
🕒 Tue-Sat: 11am-5.30pm.
Ticket prices vary.

The **Eglise St. Catherine** (Church of St. Catherine), which dates from the 14th and 15th centuries, is worth a short visit to glimpse the statue of the Black Madonna. Like many buildings in Brussels, only part of it is original. The Baroque tower is the only survivor, as the rest was replaced in the 19th century. *(Place St. Catherine, ☎ 513 34 81. 🕒 Mon-Sat: 8.30am-5pm (Summer until 6pm), Sun: 9am-12noon.)*

The unusually-coloured, Baroque **Eglise St. Jean Baptiste** (Church of St. John the

Baptist) dates from the mid- to late-17th century and is only a short walk around the corner from the Eglise St. Catherine. The exterior is a rich, beige colour, and the interior has an impressive high, vaulted roof and a striking, lavishly designed pulpit. *(Place du Beguinage, ☎ 217 87 42. ⌚ Tue: 10am-5pm, Wed-Fri: 9am-5pm, Sat (alternate) 10am-5pm, Sun 9.30am-12noon.)*

The **Monument aux Martyrs** (Monument to the Martyrs) in the middle of the rather run-down Place des Martyrs is dedicated to the 445 people who died in the revolution against the Dutch in 1830. *(Place des Martyrs.)*

The **Centre Belge de la Bande Dessinée** (Museum of the Comic Strip) is a must for anyone interested in comic strips, especially those who have read the adventures of Hergé's Tintin. The exhibits, clearly displayed and labelled, explain the history of the comic strip.

Belgium is renowned as a world leader in strip cartoons, having given us Tintin, the Smurfs and other household favourites. Adults who remember growing up with such names will enjoy the museum for nostalgic reasons and children will love it as it is full of storybook heroes.

There is also a practical exhibit on how a strip cartoon is produced from the original

Centre Belge de la Bande Dessinee

Rue des Sables
Ⓜ De Botanique
☎ 219 19 80
⌚ Tue-Sun: 10am-6pm.
Admission charge.

Comic-strip mural

L'Ilot Sacré sign

idea through to the final coloured product.

The **Colonne du Congres** (National Congress Column) was built to mark the establishment of the Belgian National Congress in 1831. Leopold I stands proudly on top of it and an eternal flame burns below as a memorial to Belgians who lost their lives in the two World Wars. *(Place du Congres.)*

Musée Charlier

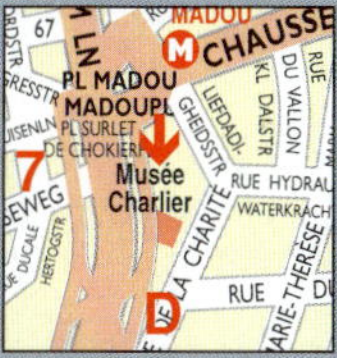

Avenue des Arts 16
Ⓜ Arts-Loi
☎ 218 53 82
🕒 Mon: 10am-5pm. Tue-Thu: 1.30pm-5pm. Fri: 1.30pm-4.30pm. Admission charge.
2 admissions for the price of 1 with voucher on page 69.

Guillame Charlier was a 19th-century artist whose works caught the eye of the wealthy art collector Henri van Cutsem. Van Cutsem agreed to be his patron and even went as far as inviting Charlier to move in to his home on Avenue des Artes. This now houses the **Musée Charlier**.

It boasts numerous fine and priceless paintings, tapestries and furniture. Some of the religious tapestries date back 400 years and yet are still in good condition. There are some excellent examples of porcelain including, on one floor, some Delftware. Almost all the pieces on display here were collected by van Cutsem and on his death Charlier inherited the lot, including the house.

The museum makes for a highly enjoyable visit and is not so big as to be

overpowering. More paintings owned by van Cutsem are displayed at another museum in the town of Tournai.

Le Botanique was put up in the early 19th century as a botanical garden. However, the palm trees and ferns were uprooted years ago and moved to the Serres Royales (Royal Hothouses, page 27). Le Botanique is now a cultural centre that regularly hosts bands, but presumably not those who play loudly enough to shatter glass. *(Rue Royale, Ⓜ Botanique, ☎ 226 12 11. ⏲ Opening times vary. Admission charge.)*

Built on the top of a hill, the **Cathédrale St. Michel et Ste. Gudule** is a marvel of architecture and building prowess that has graced the Brussels skyline for more than 400 years. Construction work began in the 13th century and took more than 300 years to complete. This long construction period means the church is a mix of several architectural styles, including Gothic and Renaissance.

Straining skyward above the main bulk of the church are its two towers which overlook the Boulevard de l'Imperatrice. The western facade is spectacular and in excellent condition following recent renovation.

Above the doors are the statues of the Three Wise Men carrying their nativity gifts and above them stand six statues of the Apostles. For the best view of the west front, approach the cathedral from the direction of the Grand Place or the Place de la Monnaie via the narrow streets and alleyways.

Inside the cathedral the 16th-century stained glass windows are

Cathédrale St. Michel et Ste. Gudule

Place St. Gudule
Ⓜ Gare Centrale
☎ 217 83 45
⏲ Mon-Sun: 8am-6pm
No visits during services.
Free, but admission charge for the crypt.
2 admissions to the crypt for the price of 1 with voucher on page 71.

Fleurs et papillons, *Musée Charlier*

Cathedral St-Michel et Ste-Gudule

magnificent, especially those depicting the Last Judgement. The crypts and the funerary monuments are masterpieces. Look out for the 'Chair of Truth', a baroque pulpit which dates from the end of the 17th century.

Although most of the major renovation work seems to have been completed on the cathedral's superstructure, with a building of this age and complexity there is always some part of it in need of attention so do not be surprised if you see scaffolding coating a wall.

Of course, the best way to see a cathedral is when it is in use, so try to attend one of the services on Saturdays and Sundays. Some are conducted in Flemish, others in French, reminding the visitor that Belgium is a bi-lingual country. The cathedral is named in honour of the patron saints of Brussels, St. Michel and St. Gudule.

Parc de Bruxelles

Rue de la Lor/Place Royale

The dukes of Brabant used to hunt on the site of the **Parc de Bruxelles** (Brussels park) but in the late 18th century the area was cleared and landscaped into formal gardens. As you walk through the park, you will come across statues at every turn and the **Royal Park Theatre** at the northern edge.

The park provides a scenic stretch if you

are strolling between the Grand Place and the Charlier Museum on Avenue des Artes, but is not the most attractive of European city parks.

The **Palais des Beaux-Arts** (Centre of Fine Arts), on Rue Ravenstein, is not much to look at from the outside – certainly no palace, even with its 1920s art deco exterior. It is, however, a leading arts centre.

Inside is a concert hall, a theatre, plenty of space for exhibitions, and a cinema museum (page 20) with a screening room which still shows silent black and white movies. There is always something going on at the Palais des Beaux-Arts and it is a popular place for lovers of the arts to meet.

Some areas are used for lectures or slide shows given by visiting speakers, and the theatre and concert hall are frequently booked up with performances, some by Brussels' main orchestras, the National and the Philharmonic. Information on what performances are being held can be obtained from the tourist information offices or the Palais itself.

The **Musée de la Dynastie** (Museum of the Royal Family) is situated in a palace called the Hôtel Bellevue on Place des Palais. It houses exhibits which trace the history of the Belgian royal family over the past 160 years. The displays comprise photographs, paintings, sculptures, and other items

Palais des Beaux-Arts

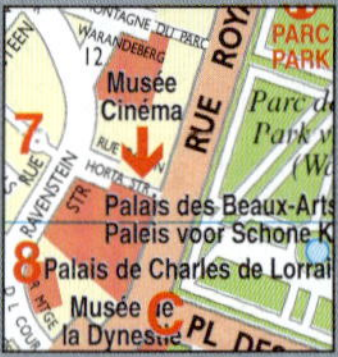

Rue Ravenstein
Ⓜ Gare Centrale
☎ 507 82 20
🕒 Tue-Sun: 10am-6pm
Admission charge.

Taking a stroll beside the Parc de Bruxelles

Gables in the Grand Place

representing different stages in the development of the monarchy.

Musée de la Dynastie

7 Place des Palais
Ⓜ Parc
☎ 511 55 78
🕒 Tue-Sun: 10am-5pm.
Mon: closed.

The **Musée du Cinema** (Cinema Museum) is a must for all cinema-goers and film buffs visiting Brussels. There are exhibits demonstrating how early cinematographic processes worked, including the technique invented by the Lumière brothers who are credited with inventing the moving image in France in 1895.

There is a whole range of magical film equipment on display and when visitors have seen the moving image being created, they can enter the screening room and watch a classic black and white silent film to see what the final product looked like. There are screenings every evening.

for less **Musée du Cinema**

9 rue Baron Horta
Ⓜ Gare Centrale
☎ 02 507 8370
🕒 Mon-Sun. Screenings: 6.30pm, 8.15pm, 10.15pm. Silent films: 7pm, 9pm.
Admission charge.
2 admissions for the price of 1 with voucher on page 69.

The 18th-century **Palais de Charles de Lorraine** (Palace of Charles of Lorraine) is charming to look at and lovingly restored inside and out. Its graceful appearance is due mainly to the foresight and artistic flair of Duke Charles de Lorraine who, in the latter half of the 18th century, commissioned the rebuilding of what had been a Gothic palace in this more modern style. Call ahead if you want a tour of the palace.

The **Bibliothèque Royale de Belgique** (Royal Library), otherwise known as the Bibliothèque Albertine, is one of the most impressive historical collections in

Brussels. It narrowly escaped destruction in a fire in the 18th century. The collected items include some exquisitely designed and produced medieval manuscripts. The library staff are only too keen to tell you how many kilometres of shelving they attend in the building (almost 100 at the last count) housing books, manuscripts and other printed materials.

As well as a sightseeing stop, the library is a working centre for research for Belgian and international academics. There is a collection of musical scores, one of prints, a room for coins and medals, a collection of up-to-date foreign newspapers and magazines, a literature museum and centres for American and African study.

The **Musée d'Art Ancien** (Museum of Ancient Art) is one of Brussels' leading museums. Despite the name, it houses a comprehensive collection of works of art which date from the 14th to the 19th centuries. The emphasis is on Dutch and Flemish masters but there are a fair number of international artists represented here too.

There is a room dedicated to the Brussels artist Pieter Breughel the Elder, which displays some of his most noted works, including *The Fall of Icarus*, *The Census of Bethlehem*, *The Adoration of the Kings*, and *Winter Landscape with Ice Skaters and Bird Trap*.

From here visitors progress into the 17th century works which include some by Rubens (*The Ascent to Calvary* and *The Martyrdom of Saint Lievin*), Jordaens (*The*

Looking towards the museum complex and Royal Library

Palais de Charles de Lorraine

Place du Musée
Ⓜ Parc
☎ 519 53 71
🕒 Groups by prior agreement.

Bibliothèque Royale de Belgique

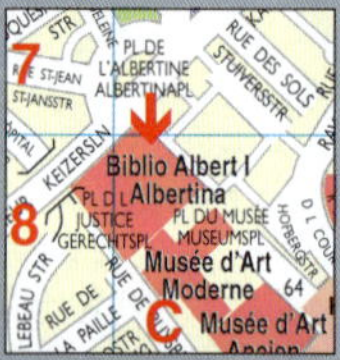

Boulevard de l Empereur
Ⓜ Gare Centrale
☎ 519 53 11
🕒 Mon-Fri: 9am-8pm, Sat: 9am-5pm.
Bring passport or ID cards to get membership card.

Palais Royale

King Drinks, Saint Martin Curing a Man Possessed and the *Allegory of Fecundity*), Van Dyck and Teniers. There is a collection of Dutch paintings from the 17th century, as well as works by Italian, French and Spanish painters.

The ground floor hosts meetings, lectures and other cultural events. Also on display is a wonderful exhibition of sculptures dating from the 19th century. including some by Rodin and Rousseau.

The museum also has the benefit of soft chairs on which to sit while you view the paintings rather than the rigid, straight backed furniture favoured by most art institutions.

The subterranean **Musée d'Art Moderne** (Museum of Modern Art) houses some of the most spectacular pieces of modern art to be produced during the 19th and 20th centuries.

The earlier works are by Belgian painters such as Ensor, Navez, Wappers, Gallait, Leys, Portaels, Stevens, De Braekeleer and Van Rysselberghe. However, those searching for the international names will discover Gauguin, Bonnard, Seurat and Signac are all represented here.

The 20th-century collection includes no less than 26 of Magritte's surrealist masterpieces and others by his contemporaries Max Ernst and Paul Delvaux. Picasso, Miró and Dali are also featured here. In other rooms visitors will

Musée d' Art Ancien

Rue de la Regence
Ⓜ Gare Centrale
☎ 508 32 11
🕒 Tue-Sun: 10am-12noon, 1pm-5pm.
Free admission.

Musée d'Art Moderne

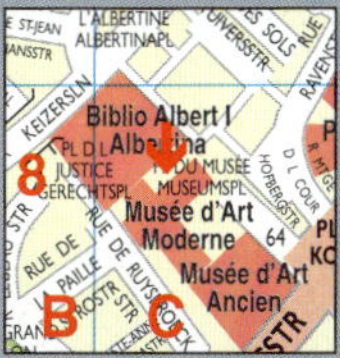

Rue de la Regence
Ⓜ Parc
☎ 508 32 11
🕒 Tue-Sun: 10am-1pm, 2pm-5pm.
Free admission.

find evidence of a comprehensive sculpture collection.

The **Palais Royale** (Royal Palace) was built on the spot where the former Palace of the Dukes of Brabant once stood. That building was burned to the ground in 1731 by the great fire. The present day Palais was started in 1820 under the watchful eye of William of Orange.

At the start of the 20th century, Leopold II ordered it be rebuilt in the style of Louis XIV. Today the Palais Royale, or the Palais du Roi (Palace of the King) as it is also known, is the city residence of the Belgian royal family when they are in town. Check with the tourist office for details on ceremonies, open days and the changing of the guard.

Situated in the Place Royale, the **Eglise St. Jacques sur Coudenberg** (Church of St. Jacques of Coudenberg) is one of Brussels most beautiful churches. It was built in 1775, and its structure represents a Roman temple. During the time of the French Revolution the church was converted into a Temple of Reason and later a Temple of the Law, but it was eventually returned to its original purpose as a place of Catholic worship in 1802. Services are worth attending and are held in French on Sundays at 5.15pm.

The **Eglise de Notre Dame au Sablon** (Church of Notre Dame in Sablon) is a good example of the exuberant Gothic

Palais Royale

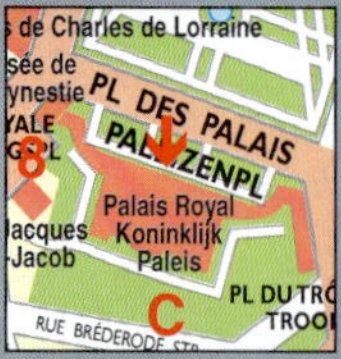

Place des Palais
Ⓜ Parc
☎ 551 20 20
🕒 Jul-Sep: Tue-Sun: 10.30am-4.30pm.

Eglise St. Jacques sur Coudenberg

Place Royale
Ⓜ Parc
☎ 511 78 36
🕒 Mon-Sat: 10am-6pm, Sun: 9am-12noon.

Flower market

Eglise de Notre Dame de la Chapelle

Rue des Ursuline
☎ 513 53 48
🕒 Jun to Sep: Sat: 9am-5pm. Sun: 1.30pm-3.30pm.
Guided tours booked in advance.

style which was widely admired in Belgium. Brussels' Guild of Crossbowmen built this particular church in the 15th century. It was constructed on the site of a 14th-century chapel which was built in honour of a small statue of the Virgin Mary which was brought here from Antwerp in 1348. The site became a centre for pilgrimage soon after. *(Rue de la Régence, Ⓜ Porte de Namur.)*

The **Musée des Postes** (Postal Museum) houses a comprehensive collection of Belgian and foreign stamps as well as examples of telecommunication machines which trace the history of the industry in this country. *(Place du Grand Sablon, Ⓜ Porte de Namur, ☎ 511 77 40. 🕒 Tue-Sat: 10am-4.30pm.)*

Musée Instrumental

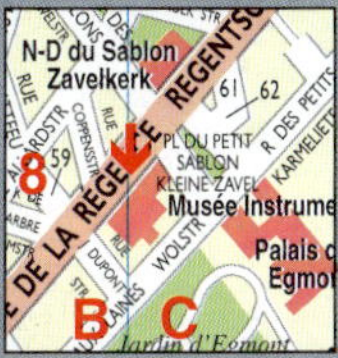

Royal Museums of Art and History
Place du Petit Sablon
☎ 511 35 95
🕒 Tue-Fri: 9.30am-4.45pm. Sat: 10am-4.45pm.
Admission charge.

Pieter Breughel the Elder was so popular in Belgium that a chapel in the **Eglise de Notre Dame de la Chapelle** (Church of Notre Dame de la Chapelle) was named after him and his wife Marie Coucke.

In another chapel, dedicated to the Holy Sacrament, a plaque commemorates Francois Anneessens, a guild leader who was beheaded in 1719 in for defending liberty. He is buried here.

The **Musée Instrumental** (Instrument Museum) is said to be one of the biggest collections of musical instruments in the world and it contains some fine specimens from across Europe. There are wind instruments from the 17th to the 19th

Palais de Justice

Ornamental architecture

centuries, keyboards of varying descriptions dating back to the 16th century, and a model of a lutemaker's workshop with examples of his craftsmanship.

There are so many instruments that the displays are rotated throughout the year. Call before visiting, as there are plans to move the museum to a new, larger location.

The **Jardin Egmont** is a popular park but its splash of greenery looks somewhat out of place in the middle of the urban surroundings. The park's centrepiece is an elaborate well called the Pollepel. *(Boulevard de Waterloo.)*

Designed by the great Brussels architect Poelaert, the **Palais de Justice** was one of the greatest monuments built in Europe in the 19th century. It was constructed in this imposing position on the top of Gallenberg Hill during the reign of Leopold II.

It acted as a reminder to all the residents of Brussels living in its mighty shadow that the law was watching them. The interior is impressive and the terrace at the front has panoramic views over the city.

The 14th-century **Porte de Hal** tower is all that remains of the second perimeter wall that surrounded Brussels. It houses the Museum of Folklore, which is currently closed until further notice.

Palais de Justice

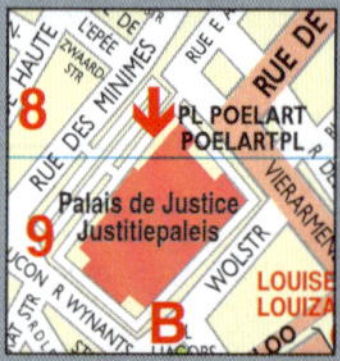

Place Poelaert,
☎ 508 64 10.
🕒 Mon-Fri: 8am-5pm.
Free admission.

Porte de Hal

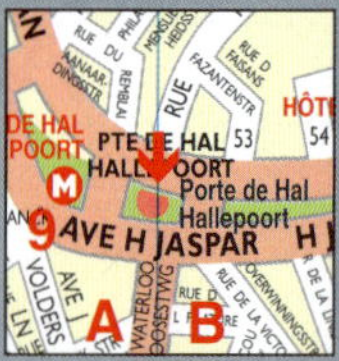

Boulevard du Midi
Ⓜ Porte de Hal
☎ 534 1518
🕒 Mon-Fri: 8am-3.30pm.
Free admission.

Northern Brussels

Basilique Nationale du Sacré Coeur

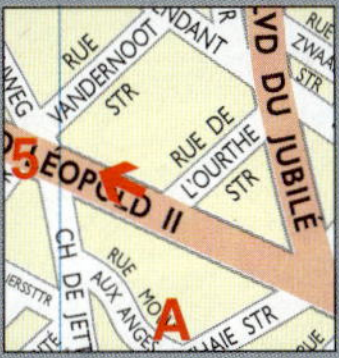

Parvis de la Basilique
Ⓜ Simonis
☎ 425 88 22
⌚ Mon-Sun: 10am-4.15pm.

One of the world's largest churches, the **Basilique Nationale du Sacré Coeur** looms above its west Brussels neighbourhood of Koekelberg like a colossus. It is located at the western end of Parc Elisabeth, where the road to Ostend and Ghent parts to circumnavigate this massive edifice. The church was built entirely in the 20th century and it is reputed to be the biggest art deco edifice ever constructed in the world.

It boasts one main dome and two smaller domed towers which look more like mini New York skyscrapers than parts of a European church. If you really want a memorable experience save your visit for Sunday at 10am when the service is accompanied by the haunting sound of the choir's Gregorian chant.

There are guided tours available but these have to be booked in advance. Visitors are allowed into the Dome from where they have one of the most spectacular views in the city.

Eglise Notre Dame de Laeken

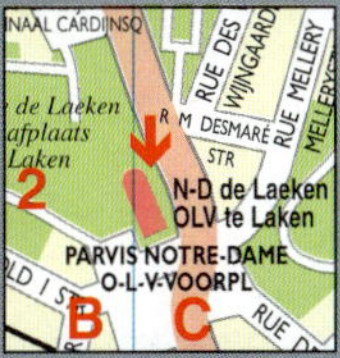

Parvis Notre Dame
Ⓜ Boek-Stael
☎ 479 23 62
⌚ Open for guided tours. Sun: 2pm-5pm. Services: times vary.

In front of the Basilique Nationale du Sacre Coeur lies the leafy **Parc Elisabeth**, which is a good place in which to relax after a lengthy stroll around the church. *(Avenue de la Liberté/Avenue de Jette, Ⓜ Simonis.)*

The church on the Parvis Notre Dame was built in the 19th century in honour of Louise-Marie, the first Queen of the Belgians. As a result, the **Eglise Notre Dame de Laeken** (Church of Notre Dame de Laeken) contains the Royal Crypt. There was an earlier church here which could be dated back to the 13th century and from which the Gothic choir stalls remain. The church also houses a copy of Rodin's *The Thinker*. Guided tours are available on Sundays but it is best to call ahead to book.

Cemetery

Parvis Notre Dame
Ⓜ Boek-Stael
☎ 479 23 62
⌚ Opening times vary according to church.

The **cemetery** of the Church of Notre Dame de Laeken holds the bones of many famous Belgians, including the dramatist Michel de Ghelderode, the architects Poelaert, Balat and Suys, and the violinist Charles de Beriot. De Beriot is buried here

with his wife, who was the opera singer known as "La Malibran".

You will find the **Château Royal** adjacent to the main royal palace in the district of Laeken to the north of the ring road. It is the residence of Queen Fabiola and entry to the public is forbidden.

The architecture of the **Serres Royales** (Royal Hothouses) in the northern district of Laeken is almost worth the trip in itself. They were put up in the 1870s, during the reign of Leopold II, who was keen to modernise the city with such grand edifices.

The expansive collections of exotic flora from around the world are excellent and need time to be admired. The pleasant climate inside the hothouses also makes them a popular destination for people in the winter months.

Visitors should check with the tourist office to see when the hothouses are open before making the trip north from the city centre.

The **Pavilion Chinois** (Chinese Pavilion) was another architectural idea of Leopold II, put up in the early part of the 20th century, which now contains exhibits of porcelain. The **Tour Japonaise** (Japanese Tower) is based on the designs of a pagoda and currently acts as a centre for

Château Royal

Avenue du Parc Royal, Laeken

Serres Royales

Avenue du Parc Royal
Ⓜ Heysel
☎ 513 89 40
🕒 Opening times vary.

Atomium

exhibitions of oriental (especially Japanese) art.

Pavillon Chinois and Tour Japonaise

Avenue van Praet
☎ 268 16 08
🕒 Tue-Sun: 10am-4.40pm.
Admission charge.

The **Atomium** must be Brussels' best known landmark. It is a giant steel structure made up of nine balls linked by struts and rising 120 metres (330 feet) above the surrounding rooftops of Heysel in north Brussels. It was built for the International Exhibition which was held here in 1958 and is a model of a metal crystalline molecule enlarged 165 billion times.

It might look a little rusty up close but it is still awe-inspiring. For a fantastic view over the city and the surrounding countryside take the elevator to the highest ball.

There is also an exhibition tracing the developments in medical science in the past century. Try to time your visit so you leave after dark when you can watch sparks of light flicking between the balls along the giant struts, resembling energy.

Atomium

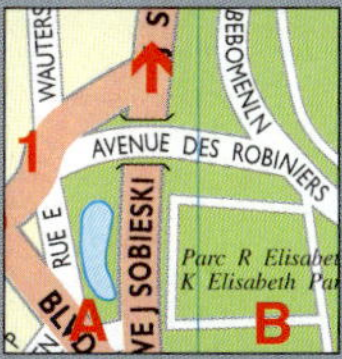

Boulevard du Centenaire
Ⓜ Heysel
☎ 474 89 77
🕒 Mon-Sun: 10am-5pm.
Admission charge.

The **Parc des Expositions** (Exhibition Park) was set aside for major exhibitions and fairs after the International Exhibition that was held here in 1958. In the past 40 years there has been no shortage of trade, and Brussels is now known as a top conference destination.

Nearby is the **Heysel Stadium** which was the scene in May 1985 of one of the worst ever football tragedies when 38 fans were killed when a wall collapsed.

Mini Europe is a theme park which gives visitors a whistle-stop tour, in miniature, of the continent. Younger travellers will get the most benefit from it but it does make an excellent family day out.

Parc des Expositions

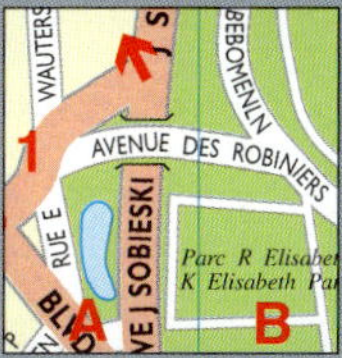

Heysel
Ⓜ Heysel

During the journey you will hear, feel, and in some cases smell the various countries of Europe. It is extraordinary in that it makes you realise just how close the individual countries are to each other and how European integration is becoming more established day by day.

There are 350 models (all of them built to scale) of Europe's most beautiful and important sites and monuments, from Brussels' own Grand Place to the Eiffel Tower, the Seville Arena, the Acropolis, Big

Mini Europe

Ben and the Leaning Tower of Pisa.

Each region has beds of its native plants to add to the realism. At certain times of the day Mount Vesuvius will erupt and high speed, pan-continental trains will clatter past. A lot of the exhibits are controlled by buttons so visitors can make things happen. The most comical include being able to make a model of a Finn run from a sauna and dive into a lake.

There are lots of useful facts on offer which should expand visitors' knowledge of Europe. You will find out how many miles a TGV train travels in a year, how long it took to create the magnificent Grand Place in Brussels' city centre, and why gondolas in Venice are always painted black.

Aside from the fun there is a historical aspect to Mini Europe. It offers a snapshot heritage lesson on individual countries and the continent as a whole and how its internal boundaries have shifted – often violently – over the past centuries.

There are several festivals staged at different times of the year and concentrating on particular countries or cultures. Visitors should call ahead for a brochure or check with the tourist office in the city centre to see what's on and when.

Mini Europe

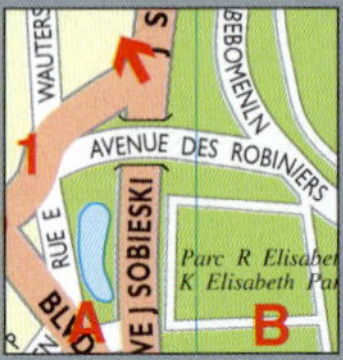

Bruparck, Boulevard du Centenaire
Ⓜ Heysel
☎ 478 05 50
🕒 Mon-Sun: 9.30pm-6pm (until 8pm at times in summer).
Admission charge.

East Brussels

Parliament

Parc Leopold

Rue Belliard
Ⓜ Schuman

The **Parc Leopold** (Leopold Park) is one of Brussels' smaller and prettier parks. It is situated on a steep slope near the **Parliament** building and makes a good spot for a stroll if visitors want to take a break from sightseeing. The main entrance is found on Rue Belliard.

If you are aware of Antoine Wiertz' work then you will know what to expect, but for those who are not familiar with his paintings and sculptures, watch out for some powerful exhibits at the **Musée Antoine Wiertz**.

Musée Antoine Wiertz

Rue Vautier
Ⓜ Trone
☎ 648 17 18
🕒 Tue-Fri: 10am-noon, 1pm-5pm.

Wiertz (1806-1865) aspired to be a great artist and produced works of great passion, many of them painted on vast canvasses deliberately to impress critics and the public. He did not make it into the top flight but is remembered fondly by devotees all the same. He was deeply influenced by the Renaissance, yet a lot of his subject matter would fit better into the surreal canvasses of Dali or Bosch.

Some of his works have been described as deeply macabre and the result of a twisted mind and wicked imagination. A look around the Musée Antoine Wiertz can certainly be a strange experience.

The **Museum de l'Institut Royal des Sciences Naturelles** (Museum of Natural Sciences) houses a comprehensive display

of dinosaur bones and numerous other exhibits from all sectors of the natural world.

Among the permanent exhibitions is one dealing with fossils and how they tell us vital information about evolution and the development of vertebrates. It also focuses on the widely believed genetic links between dinosaurs and birds.

There are some examples of ancient marine lizards, and a large section on insects and how they affect their environments. The African termite mound is always popular with children.

With increasing concern being voiced over the earth's oceans and coral reefs, the museum's section on shells is especially relevant. Part of this section is comprised of an aquarium, which displays some rare and tropical species of fish. There are also skeletons and models of the giants of the deep for visitors to examine and marvel at.

There is a separate section on mammals and another which concentrates on the wildlife of Belgium.

Finally there is a display of minerals and gems including an exhibit of beautiful crystals, fragments of moon rocks and meteorites that have crashed to earth. Many of these minerals have actually been discovered here in Belgium.

Give yourself a good half-day to look

Museum de l'Institut Royal des Sciences Naturelles

Chaussee de Wavre 226
Trone
☎ 627 42 38
Tue-Fri: 9.30am-4.45pm. Sat-Sun: 10am-6pm.
Admission charge.
2 admissions for the price of 1 with voucher on page 71.

Museum de l'Institut Royal des Sciences Naturelles

around the museum and call ahead if you intend to bring a group or require a guided tour.

Residence Palace

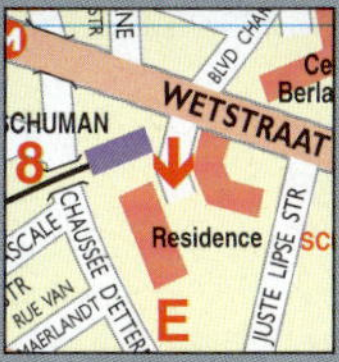

Rue de la Loi
Ⓜ Schuman
☎ 231 03 05

The **Residence Palace** is a stunning Art Deco building erected in the early 1900s and ranging over 11 floors. It contains a private swimming pool and a working theatre. The Council of Europe has some offices in the Residence now.

The **Rond Point Schumann** (Schumann Roundabout) is the heart of euro-politics. It is where diplomats and eurocrats, journalists and lobbyists live and work. Perhaps unsurprisingly in the land of the unlimited expense account, it is renowned as an excellent place to dine out and has restaurants serving cuisines from across the continent. The dominant building is the rather ugly **Centre Berlaymont**, built in 1967.

Rond Point Schumann

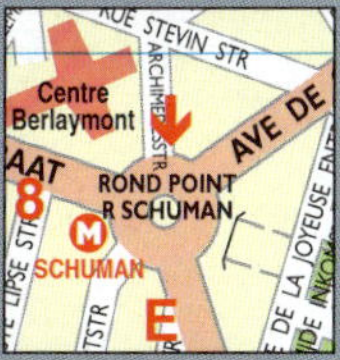

Rue de la Loi and Parc du Cinquantenaire, Etterbeek
Ⓜ Schuman

The roundabout is situated between the Rue de la Loi and the **Parc du Cinquantenaire** (Fifty Years Park). This park was designed and laid out in 1880 to host an exhibition commemorating Belgium's 50 years of independence.

As you walk through it you will spot eight statues of women who represent the eight provinces of this small nation. It is a useful place to take a break if the sightseeing is getting too much for you.

Any visitors interested in military history should make time to walk around the

Centre Berlaymont

Parc du Cinquantenaire

Musée Royal de l'Armee (Royal Museum of the Army) in the Parc du Cinquantenaire. It is said to be one of the largest military museums in the world. There are exhibits showing a wide range of weapons dating as far back as the 8th century and including swords, suits of armour, shields and helmets. Some of the more recent exhibits include weapons used during the Belgian Revolution in 1830.

There are Belgian Army uniforms and hoards of field equipment preserved from the end of the 19th and beginning of the 20th centuries. Separate sections look at the advances in ground and air transport during times of conflict.

As visitors progress through the museum so the exhibits become more up-to-date. Machine guns and other automatic weapons are laid out alongside displays from the First and Second World Wars. These two displays are particularly poignant and remind the visitor what a great price the Belgians paid in both conflicts as so much of the fighting took place on their soil.

The museum is also well illustrated with collections of photographs, maps, posters and other military memorabilia and can provide guided tours if notified in advance.

Also known as the Cinquantenaire Museum, the **Musées Royaux d'Art et d'**

Parc du Cinquantenaire

Avenue de Tervuren & Rue de la Loi
Ⓜ Schuman

Musée Royal de l'Armee

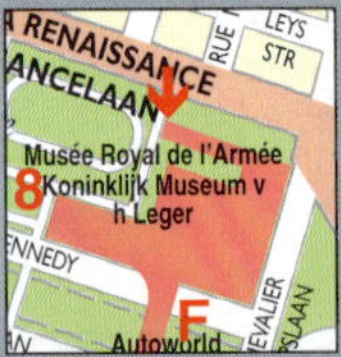

Parc du Cinquantenaire
Ⓜ Schuman
☎ 733 44 93
🕒 Tue-Sun: 10am-4.45pm. Mon: 10am-4.45pm.

Histoire (Royal Museums of Art and History) in the Parc du Cinquantenaire are filled with artefacts collected from the ancient civilisations of southern Europe and the Middle East.

The Roman and Egyptian exhibits are particularly worth seeing. There is an antiquity section which covers these comprehensively, as well as examining the skills of Greek craftsmen and ceramicists. Look out for the beautiful mosaic from Apamea in Syria and a range of intricate objects from Mesopotamia.

Items from further afield, notably India, South East Asia and the Americas, can be found in the exhibit entitled Non-European Civilisations.

In the National Archaeology section visitors can see how people have lived in this lush, wooded region of northern Europe from Roman times to the present day.

The fourth and final section of the museum is dedicated to the decorative arts. You can follow the progression of this art form from the Middle Ages to the 20th century through sculpture, furniture, ceramics. The evolution of tapestries and lacework is also covered. Belgium became a World-leader in both of these art forms in the 17th century.

If your interest in cars is limited to driving them to work and back then **Autoworld**, in the Parc du Cinquantenaire, will appear as little more than a giant aircraft hangar full of hunks of shining metal. If, on the other hand, you are one of those people for whom cars represent the height of design excellence and industrial achievement then Autoworld is a must-see.

The collection of approximately 400 cars contains some real classics. The vast metal structure with its arched roof like a railway station was put up at the end of the 19th century to house the annual motor shows, which were held in Belgium between 1900 and the 1930s.

The exhibits proclaim that Belgium played a key role in the manufacturing of cars during the first half of the 20th century, although the national trade names might

Musées Royaux d'Art et d'Histoire

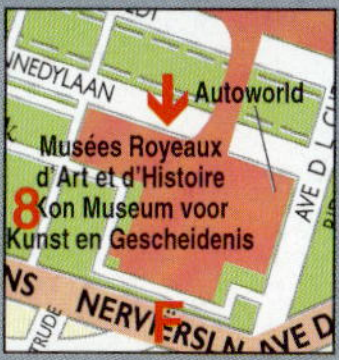

Parc du Cinquantenaire
Ⓜ Schuman
☎ 741 72 11
Tue-Fri: 9.30am-5pm. Sat-Sun: 10am-5pm. Admission charge.

Autoworld

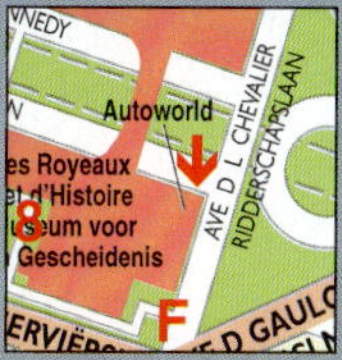

Parc du Cinquantenaire
Ⓜ Merode
☎ 736 41 65
Apr-Sep: Mon-Sun: 10am-6pm. Oct-Mar: Mon-Sun: 10am-5pm. Admission charge.

Musée des Enfants

Rue de Bourgmestre 15
☎ 640 01 07
Wed, Sat, Sun and school holidays: 2.30pm-5pm. Aug: closed. Admission charge.
2 admissions for the price of 1 with voucher on page 69.

not be as well known and those of other nationalities.

Among the foreign cars are a wonderful early Volkswagen Beetle and a Model T Ford. Parked among the 1930s-style streetlights are a number of celebrities' cars, including one designed for the former US President John F Kennedy.

The **Musée des Enfants** (Children's Museum) is a bright and welcome concept, more a journey of discovery than a museum. It involves every child that enters it, and plenty of adults too, by requiring them to take part in activities including cooking, painting and role-playing.

Children can learn about the world around them and undertake almost any role, be it a farmer or a space explorer. It is great fun as well as being informative for youngsters aged between 4 and 12, and it teaches important skills such as teamwork and cooperation.

The exhibits and workshops, which are based around particular themes, change every so often, so call ahead to find out what is currently on display. The tourist office should also have the latest details.

Horse-drawn carriages, trams and buses are all on display in the fascinating **Musée de Transport Urbain Bruxellois** (Urban Transport Museum) which concentrates on public transport in the city.

Musée de Transport Urbain Bruxellois

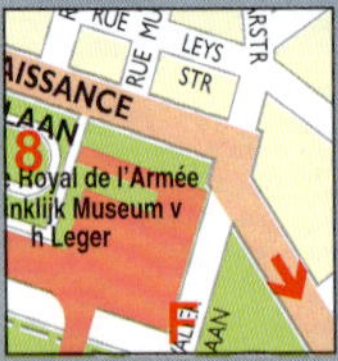

Avenue de Tevuren 364B
☎ 515 31 08
Apr-Sep: Sat, Sun and Public Holidays: 1.30pm-7pm.
Admission charge.
2 admissions for the price of 1 with voucher on page 67.

Autoworld

The exhibits stretch back to the 1860s when commuting to work might actually have been pleasurable, at least compared with today. Horse-drawn trams gave way to ones propelled by steam engines, but soon even they were not powerful enough and the race was on to develop faster transport. Bigger engines were brought in and eventually ones were developed that used electricity and carried hooks that connected them to live current running through wires overhead. Visitors to the museum can take a trip on an old electric tram.

Château Malou

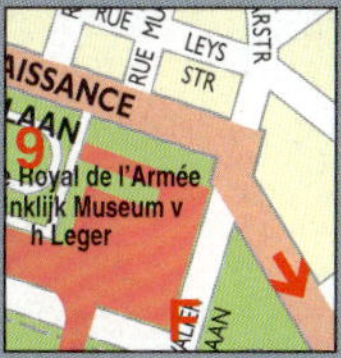

Chaussee de Stockel
☎ 761 27 66
🕒 Open only during exhibitions.

Klimt was one of several artists who worked on the magnificent exterior of the **Palais Stocklet** between 1905 and 1911. The abstract design incorporates marble, bronze and wrought-iron. Unfortunately, when this 20th-century palace was opened to the public it was discovered that visitors had taken a number of the exhibits, so it is now closed. *(279-281 Avenue de Tervuren. 🕒 Not open to the public.)*

The beautiful 18th-century **Château Malou** is the base for a cultural centre and an art gallery. As its name suggests, it is situated in the attractive surroundings of the Parc Malou. Both are named after the Malou family who were the former owners and residents. It is now in the hands of the city authorities. Exhibits and opening times vary so check in advance.

Musée des Enfants

South and West Brussels

Toulouse-Lautrec's famous Paris posters

The **Maison d'Ecrivains Belges de Langue Français** (Centre for French speaking Belgian writers) will no doubt have its critics but it is nevertheless an interesting place to visit. There is a replica of a writer's garret as well as a small collection of writing paraphernalia and memorabilia. It is situated in a pretty town house which dates from the end of the 19th century.

The **Musée Communal d'Ixelles** (Ixelles Museum) is one of Brussels' best art museums. The walls are lined with copies of flamboyant, colourful posters by Toulouse-Lautrec who so accurately captured the spirit of Paris's demi-monde. His works light up the museum, showing beautiful, lithe dancers on flimsy stages and bawdy bars full of merry-making.

Although there are works of art on display which date from the 16th through to the 18th century, the selection of 20th century works is the most interesting. There are paintings from a wide variety of schools of art – from symbolism to surrealism and impressionism to pop art. It is one of the more manageable museums of art in the city and is ideal if you are on a short visit.

Maison d'Ecrivains Belges de Langue Français

Chaussee de Wavre

Musée Communal d'Ixelles

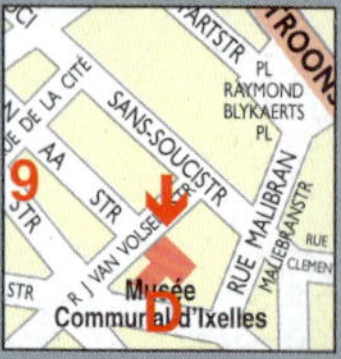

Rue Jean van Volsem
☎ 511 90 84
🕒 Tue-Fri: 1pm-6.30pm.
Sat, Sun: 10am-5pm.
Admission charges vary.

Musée Horta

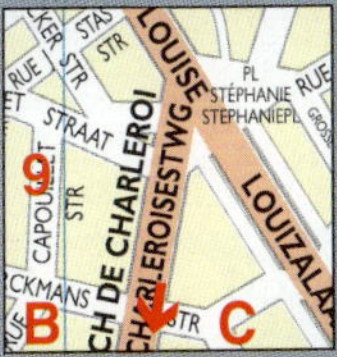

Rue Americaine
☎ 543 04901
🕒 Tue-Fri and every second Sat-Sun: 10am-12noon, 1pm-5pm. Mon: closed.

Victor Horta, the famous Belgian architect lived and worked in what is now the **Musée Horta** (Horta Museum). The building was designed and built at the end of the 19th and beginning of the 20th century in the elegant but eccentric Art Nouveau style for which Horta was famous.

Take time to examine the stained glass windows, the mosaics and the furniture. Many of them possess the fluidity that Horta so cherished and strove to portray. There is also a collection of paintings and murals.

Fans of Horta or those who have studied his work academically will delight in the small but useful research centre that exists here. Possibly most illuminating of all is the collection of blueprints which were drawn up by Horta for some of his best known buildings. He designed, among others, the Palais des Beaux Artes (page 19).

Musée Constantin Muenier

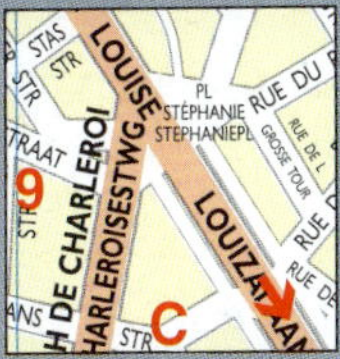

59 rue de l'Abbaye
☎ 648 4449
🕒 Tue-Fri: 1pm-7pm. Sat-Sun: 10am-5pm.

The **Musée Constantin Muenier** (Constantin Muenier Museum) is housed in the studio where the painter and sculptor Constantin Muenier lived and worked during the latter half of the 19th century. Most of a collection of almost 800 works that he left when he died in 1905 are displayed here. Some of the watercolours and sketches are of a particularly high quality.

The **Abbaye de la Cambre** was founded for

An ornate house sign

It is a pleasant tram ride to Tervuren

the Citeaux order of nuns in the 13th century. Today the abbey's buildings are the headquarters of the National Geographic Institute and also house an arts centre. The **Eglise Notre Dame de la Cambre** is a 16th century church attached to the abbey. Both buildings are attractively lit after dark, and are surrounded by beautiful gardens where visitors can rest.

Beyond the gardens of the old abbey and church lie the extensive **Bois de la Cambre** (La Cambre Woods). They cover an area of 124 hectares (500 acres) and form part of the former woodland known as the **Forest of Soignes**. Today the woods are extremely popular for recreation and provide a playground for numerous outdoor activities from roller-skating to horse riding. In the summer months outdoor concerts are staged here among the trees.

The collection of artefacts in the **Musée Royal d'Afrique** (Royal African Museum) in Tervuren reflects the rich diversity of religions and cultures in Central Africa. There are some impressive masks and statues, and a display of flora and fauna from this part of the world.

There are mementoes from the time of Belgian colonial expansion in Africa as well as records of important archaeological finds. *(Chaussee de Louvain, Tervuren, ☎ 769 52 11. ⌚ Tue-Fri: 10am-5pm. Sat-Sun: 10am-6pm. Admission charge.)*

Abbaye de la Cambre

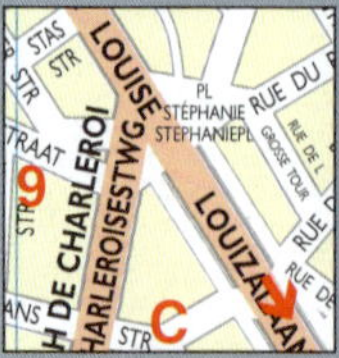

Avenue E. Duray
☎ 648 1121
⌚ Mon-Fri: 9am-12noon, 2pm-6pm. Sat: 3pm-6pm. Sun: 8am-12.30pm, 3pm-6pm (except during services). Catholic feast days: 9am-12noon.

Bois de la Cambre

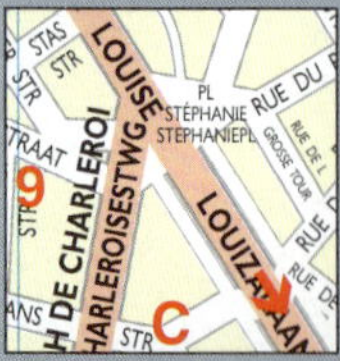

Avenue Louise

Musée David et Alice van Buuren

The **Musée David et Alice van Buuren** (Museum of David and Alice van Buuren) is an excellent way to see just how lavishly the rich were able to live in the early part of the 20th century.

David van Buuren was a wealthy Dutch banker and, with his wife Alice, paid a good deal of care and attention to the design, construction and decoration of their sumptuous Brussels home and the gardens that surround it. The interior is unmistakably art deco which reflects the mood of the period in which it was built.

The van Buurens spared no expense and delighted in using the most exotic and luxurious of materials, such as ivory and tropical hardwoods, to decorate their palatial domain. There is also an art collection in the house which contains a version of the Fall of Icarus painted by Pieter Breughel the Elder.

The gardens stretch away from the house for roughly 1.2 hectares (3 acres) and are well worth a visit. Tour groups are admitted but only by prior arrangement.

The **Eglise des Sts Pierre et Guidon** (Church of St. Peter and St. Guido) is one of the oldest churches in Brussels. It is said that parts of its foundations date back to the 10th century. However, the present building originates from between the 14th and 16th centuries and the spire is even younger, being less than 200 years old. It is an excellent example of Gothic architecture.

The crypt retains the sarcophagus of St. Guidon which has been dated to either

Musée David et Alice van Buuren

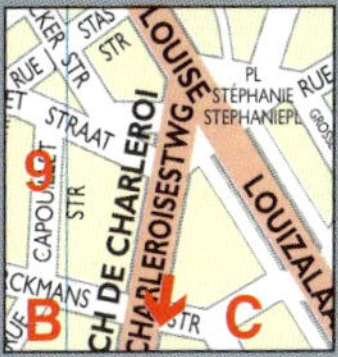

Avenue Leo Errera
☎ 343 48 51
Mon: 2pm-4pm. Sun 1pm-6pm. Garden: Mon-Sun: 2pm-6pm.
Admission charge.
2 admissions for the price of 1 with voucher on page 67.

the 11th or 12th century. Of particular interest are the well-preserved medieval wall paintings.

Eglise des Sts Pierre et Guidon

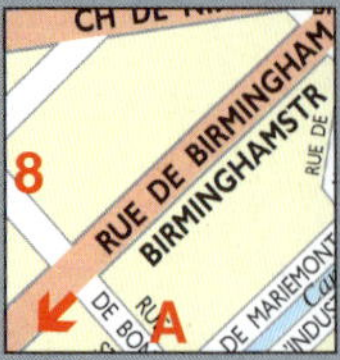

Place de la Vaillance
Ⓜ St. Guidon
☎ 521 84 15
🕒 Mon-Fri: 9am-12noon, 2.30pm-6pm.

The **Musée Erasmus** (Erasmus House Museum) traces the development throughout the continent of a wide range of cultural, religious and political movements over the ages. It is named after the Dutch Renaissance humanist Desiderius Erasmus who stayed here in 1521.

Erasmus, who lived from 1466 to 1536, strove for the reform of the Roman Catholic church and heavily criticised traditional forms of teaching. There are collections of furniture, books, engravings and other works of art which refer back to various stages in the evolution of Europe, through the Renaissance, the Humanist movement, the development of the printed word and periods of religious turbulence.

In the reading room visitors will find a comprehensive collection of manuscripts and volumes from the Middle Ages but prior notice must be given to view these. Also on display are original editions of *In Praise of Folly*, one of Erasmus's greatest works which is still widely read. The house recently underwent considerable renovation and is now one of Brussels' most important museums.

Musée Erasmus

31 Rue de Chapitre
Ⓜ St. Guidon
☎ 521 13 83
🕒 Mon, Wed, Thu, Sat, Sun: 10am-12noon, 2pm-5pm.
Admission charge.
2 admissions for the price of 1 with voucher on page 69.

Musée Erasmus

Bruges

Bruges is a fascinating and extremely picturesque town, just an hour's train ride north of Brussels.

Thankfully the German bombs missed Bruges in the Second World War – mainly because the Luftwaffe were determined to push on to the North Sea coast and cripple the major ports like Rotterdam and Antwerp.

As a result, the town has been remarkably preserved. It looks not unlike it did back in the Middle Ages when, commercially, it was living through its boom time.

Bruges was renowned around the world for the quality and designs of its cloth. Visiting merchants who bought the cloth took it home to their native countries and were soon sent back to fetch more.

As a result of the city's commercial success, the world's first stock exchange opened here . It was a crude affair at first, a place to change money in front of the **House der Beurze** on Vlamingstrat. Later, a handsome building was erected to house the financial transactions.

Much of the cloth was sold from stalls which were sheltered by the roofs of an

The Belfrey, Bruges

Market Square, Bruges

enclosed square off the **Grote Markt** (Main Square).

The **Belfry**, which dominates the Grote Markt, is a good place to start your tour. Take your time climbing the 366 steps to the top.

On the way up you can stop off and admire the fiendishly complex workings of the giant mechanical clock. It has a satisfying tick until it gets close to the hour, when levers start being pulled and cogs start spinning automatically before the bells at the very top of the tower announce the time across the rooftops.

If you can stand the noise – and the crowds – try to get to the Belfry for midday. The view is spectacular and being able to see the streets laid out beneath will help you get your bearings.

The red terracotta roofs might make you think you are in a town in Provence or Spain but as soon as the chill wind from the North Sea starts blowing you will remember where you are. The Mediterranean influence was left by the Spanish who once ruled the region.

At night the Belfry and its adjacent buildings in the Grote Markt are beautifully lit and shine orange against the night sky. Beneath them flutter large flags bearing the coats of arms of the city and the region.

Reflections

'Somewhere within the dingy casing lay the ancient city like a notorious jewel' - Graham Greene on Bruges

A trip on the canal

You can sit in one of the many bars and restaurants in the square, eat North Sea mussels, sip Belgian beer and marvel at the glorious architecture.

On the canals, tour operators run short history cruises in a variety of languages. Check with the tourist office for the best tour as some can be brief and uninformative. Also, don't be surprised if the canals are a bit smelly, especially if you are visiting Bruges during the summer months.

Reflections

'In Bruges, assailed on every side by the picturesque, you look curiously for the unpicturesque and do not find it' – Arnold Bennett, 1896

The **Burg**, or Old Town Square, is surrounded by the most ornate buildings in Bruges, including the **Heilig Bloed Basiliek** (Basilica of the Holy Blood). For many Catholics it is an essential sight to visit but it is still fascinating whatever your religion.

A small phial kept behind protective glass within a bejewelled tabernacle is said to contain a few drops of Christ's blood. On Ascension Day each year the tabernacle is taken from its chapel and paraded through the streets with great pomp and ceremony. Scenes from passion plays are performed and legends told.

At all times of the year there is a long line of people waiting inside the building to receive a blessing from one of the priests here.

Bruges is now so popular with tourists that it can become crowded, especially in summer, and nowhere is this more obvious than at the **Onze Lieve Vrouwekerk**, the church which contains Michelangelo's *Madonna and Child* statue.

Visitors sometimes have to wait quite a while to get in, and the church has recently employed staff to tell people to be quiet if they are a little over-enthusiastic about Michelangelo's artistic wizardry.

The church's tower is almost 122 metres (400 feet) high and its spire is 37 metres (130 feet), making it easily identifiable from virtually every street in the town.

Art lovers should head for the **Memling Museum** on Mariastraat and the **Groeninge Museum** on the Dijver for some of the most beautiful examples of Flemish painting.

The former houses works by Hans Memling, a German painter who lived in Bruges from 1465 to 1494, while the latter contains a collection of works by various Flemish masters including Jan Van Eyck and Emile Claus.

In the nearby **Gruuthuse Museum**, also on Dijver, hang a collection of well preserved 17th-century tapestries and a collection of lace.

If by this time you are feeling hungry, Bruges has scores of restaurants. Being only a few miles from the North Sea coast,

Grote Markt

A windmill near Bruges

seafood is very good. Popular local dishes include Flemish cod, which is steamed with potatoes and green vegetables, and *snails bourguignonne* (snails roasted with garlic).

Mussels are a Bruges speciality as well, and come in a huge steaming bowl with a hunk of bread.

And, of course, there is beer. In some bars you will find menus detailing more than 300 different types. If, after a big lunch all you want is a snack with your evening drink, most bars can provide a plate of smoked cheese or paté and some bread.

It seems that everyone cycles in Bruges. Cars are all but banned from the main square and rush hour is a cacophony of bicycle bells. So hiring a bicycle for the day is easy and cheap – sometimes free, as some hotels offer free cycle hire – and always worthwhile because riding around Bruges and its environs is untaxing and fun.

One popular ride will take you around the perimeter of the city centre along the canals that encircle it. On the north-east stretch are the famous windmills, which are among Bruges most popular landmarks. At least one of them still works and is open to the public.

A few miles to the north of the town is the pretty inland port of **Damme** – another masterpiece of medieval architecture. The ride under the poplar trees along the towpath of the main canal from Bruges to the North Sea makes a relaxing and enjoyable day out.

Antwerp

Two words – diamonds and art – draw visitors to **Antwerp**. It is a short train ride from Brussels and, although it is not the most picturesque of places, it is Belgium's second city, boasts the country's largest port, and in recent years has smartened itself up through inner city renewal programmes and an emphasis on culture.

The Flemish master painter Pieter Paul Rubens, after being born in exile, returned to Antwerp with his family in 1587 and lived and worked here. Some of his most famous works are distributed around the city's public buildings. Four hang in the **Onze Lieve Vrouwekathedraal**, a fine Gothic church, and there others in the **Museum Plantin-Moretus**, the **Rockoxhuis Museum**, and a few in the **Rubenshuis** (Ruben's House) itself.

It is best to start exploring Antwerp from the centre, the **Grote Markt**, where the **Brabo Fountain** is a popular meeting places for friends. The **Nationaal Scheepvaartmuseum** (National Maritime Museum) has interesting displays which trace the history of shipping and the role that Antwerp has played as a world port.

Antwerp also put itself on the map by becoming a leading world centre of the diamond trade. The **Diamond District** is centred in the streets around **Centraal Station**. This area at first looks far too run-down to host such a lucrative industry but perhaps that is all part of the plan by the shrewd diamond traders. The **Diamantmuseum** (Diamond Museum) on Lange Herentalsestraat gives visitors a good introduction to this secretive world, explaining how the diamonds are mined, transported, cut and sold.

Reflections

'As Antwerp goes, so goes the rest of Belgium a few years later' – Belgian saying

Antwerp

Ghent

Like Bruges, **Ghent** grew rich from the cloth trade. The industry flourished here during the 13th and 14th centuries and traders came from numerous foreign lands to purchase the famous designs. However, it is different from Bruges in one particular way. There are no queues for monuments here. Ghent is certainly not on the tourist trail and a trip here makes a pleasant change from the constant ringing of cash registers in Bruges and Brussels.

Among the sights is **St. Baafskathedraal** (St. Baaf's Cathedral) in St. Baafsplein. The church is dramatic inside with high arches supported by elegant columns of stone, and surprisingly light for a heavy Gothic structure.

Near St. Baaf's Cathedral is **Lakenhalle**, the former centre of the cloth industry which once buzzed with activity as traders bought and sold, and vast lengths of material were carted to and fro amid the throngs of people. The hall has a **Belfry** like the one at Bruges which can be climbed for magnificent views over the rooftops.

Did You Know...?

In its 19th century heyday, Ostend was so upmarket and elite that Queen Victoria holidayed here.

It is worth seeking out the **Graslei**, a street down by the harbour which is made up of a row of well preserved **guild houses** that date back to the Middle Ages. Each building housed a different guild and they were identified by carvings, the remains of which are still visible in the weather-beaten stonework. Down here by the harbour visitors get a good sense of what dock life must have been like.

To understand how brutal life was in the Middle Ages, take a tour around the macabre torture chambers of the **Het Gravensteen**, a well preserved 12th century castle which was once owned and inhabited by the Counts of Flanders.

Internationally renowned painters such as Hieronymous Bosch, Jacob Jordaens, Pieter Paul Rubens and Van Dyck are all represented in the city's art galleries and museums. The tourist office will be able to give more information on which artists' paintings are where.

Ostend

Ostend has had a rough press in the past. It has been criticised for being a cold, wet, northern town blasted for much of the year by the cruel waves and winds of the North Sea. But during the summer months Ostend comes alive.

The **James Ensorhuis** (house of the painter James Ensor) on Vlaanderenstraat has recently reopened after much restoration and offers an interesting hour's tour.

The giant **Casino** on the seafront hosts regular concerts by travelling rock groups and classical orchestras.

The streets are packed with restaurants, some of them of a high quality. Mussels, lobster and a dish of eels in green parsley sauce are all popular local specialities. And there are, as there are everywhere in Belgium, scores of bars serving hundreds of beers almost 24 hours a day.

Ostend used to be the most glamorous of destinations. Victorian Englishmen and women in the 19th century boarded steamers and came across the English Channel to parade along the elegant promenade. It was considered the most stylish place in Europe. Times have changed and now it has lost much of its glamour but it is still fun to hire out a four-person **bicycle-buggy** and pedal along the front.

On most days there is an open-air market near the Nordzee channel where the huge ferries pull in and discharge their passengers. It sells dried fish to eat and fragile sea urchin shells to take home as mementoes. The Aquarium, which is located nearby, is interesting and only takes half an hour to view.

Ostend

Dining

A tantalising display of fruit and vegetables

Place Ste. Catherine

Ⓜ Ste. Catherine

Toone VII
Bar / Café

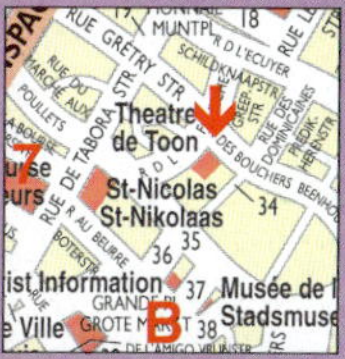

6 impasse Schuddeveld,
Petite rue des Bouchers
Ⓜ Bourse
☎ 511 7137

Eating out in Brussels or the other major Belgian towns can be an awe-inspiring experience. It can also be more expensive than visitors initially think, so it pays to do some research into the most reasonable places.

In the spring the Belgians prepare hop shoots and croquettes of shrimps coated in breadcrumbs and deep-fried to a crisp. Or they eat a delicious chicken stew which is known locally as *waterzooi*.

In early summer you will find herrings on the menu, fresh from the North Sea and tenderly cooked. By the time autumn begins to lower the temperatures, the Belgian favourite *moules frites* (mussels with french fries) become widely available, along with rabbit and partridge stews.

Whatever time of year you decide to visit Brussels you will find sumptuous menus awaiting you.

The **Place Ste. Catherine** and its adjacent streets (known as the Fish Market) is a popular area for seafood restaurants which serve anything from lobster and oysters from the coast to giant flat fish from deeper waters. Expect to pay more in the obviously touristy places here and especially in the streets around the **Grand Place**.

Le Sablon is another district of Brussels known for its gastronomy. Here you will find a host of smaller cafés and bars as well as more formal restaurants.

If you want to mix with the diplomats and Eurocrats, then head for the **Etterbeek** district where the EU movers and shakers work and play. Unsurprisingly this area is awash with fine restaurants serving dishes from all over the continent to satisfy homesick politicians, lawyers and journalists.

As with many European capital cities, meat does seem to dominate the menu. Fish is a good alternative but strict vegetarians will have a difficult time. Check with the tourist office for the best vegetarian restaurants. There are doubtless more opening as we write this guide.

Then of course there are the chocolates. Belgium produces arguably the finest chocolates in the world, some of them so exclusive they come individually wrapped in ribbons and tied up with a bow.

Café culture is very much *de rigueur* in Brussels and you do not have to walk far in this city to find exquisite bars where you can spend a half-hour lingering over an espresso and a small cake.

If you like spending time in friendly bars, you will enjoy Brussels. Le Sablon is one of the trendiest areas for café-hopping but the Grand Place has a wide selection too. There are Irish bars playing tapes of fiddle music and serving Guinness, Latin American bars with live salsa dancing and exotic daiquiris, elegant French cafés that look more like those of the Champs Elysees, and there is even a British pub or two.

Comme Chez Soi
European Restaurant

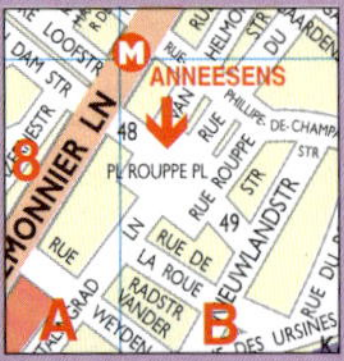

23 place Rouppe
Ⓜ Annessens
☎ 512 29 21

Horta Brasserie
Café / Restaurant

Rue des Sables
Ⓜ De Botanique
☎ 217 7271

A Bruges café

Shopping

Window shopping

The main concentrations of shops in Brussels are around the **Place de la Monnaie**, the **Rue A. Dansaert** and, of course, the **Grand Place**.

Most shops tend to open from 10am to 6pm or 7pm, or later in the summer months. Some department stores will stay open until 9pm or 10pm at weekends. Sunday opening is also catching on.

Many visitors will want to take home a lavishly priced box of mouth-watering chocolate pralines or a box of sugar-coated biscuits. If beer is your poison then you may never leave Brussels. The choice is immense (several hundred different brands) and they are all too prevalent in shop windows to be sold by the bottle, box, or crate, all very cheap by European standards.

If you can drag yourself away from beer and chocolate then a fine piece of Brussels lace would make an excellent gift. The city was once a world leader in lace making. Hundreds of women created delicate masterpieces which were sought out by nobility and wealthy families from all over the world.

If money is no object then take a tour around the antique shops of **Le Sablon**. You might find a bargain. Some have beautiful copies of medieval Belgian tapestries. The **Galeries St. Hubert** shopping arcade, reputed to be the first covered shopping street in Europe, is a great place for window shopping.

If you find yourself in **Antwerp**, a world centre for the diamond trade, you might cast your eye over the prices. Most will be

Place de la Monnaie

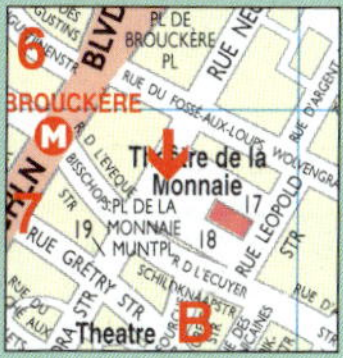

Ⓜ De Brouckère

Inno
Department Store

111 rue Neuve
Ⓜ De Brouckère
☎ 219 02 90

phenomenally expensive but you can always window shop.

One of Brussels' most endearing characters is the cartoon boy hero Tintin, and the city's merchandisers have made sure the world knows about it. There are Tintin mugs, postcards, pencil sharpeners, posters, bags, balloons and miniature models of the rocket in which he went to the moon. Tintin's faithful dog Snowy also has a line of goods all to himself. They make great presents for friends or mementoes for yourself.

Brussels' long association with the comic strip means there are many shops around the city which sell nothing else. There are also scores of bookshops: second-hand, antiquarian, French, Flemish, and international.

As far as clothes are concerned, there are the usual expensive, designer-label shops here as well as more affordable outlets, but the prices are little different from elsewhere in Europe or North America.

The street markets are great places to people-watch. The area around the **Place du Grand Sablon** hosts a market selling coins and stamps at weekends, and in the Grand Place there is a flower market every morning. Both are good for browsing and for photography. For a truly vast market go to the **Gare du Midi** on Sunday mornings where you can pick up a week's food shopping as well as flowers and records.

Place du Grand Sablon

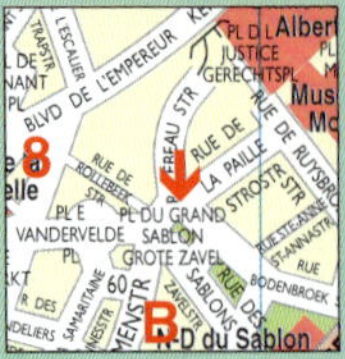

Ⓜ Gare Centrale

Privé Joke
Designer Clothes

8 rue des Riches Claires
Ⓜ Bourse
☎ 502 73 68

Shopping for bargains

Théâtre de la Monnaie

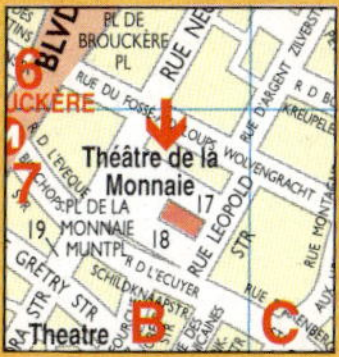

Place de la Monnaie,
Rue Leopold
Ⓜ De Brouckère
☎ 229 12 11

Nightlife

There are hundreds of bars and cafés in Brussels scattered around the city. It is confusing to know which to visit so check with the tourist offices or the front desk staff at your hotel, as the range of options can be baffling.

There are old, weather-beaten cafés with paint peeling off the walls and grumpy waitresses, yet bursting with character; there are brand new bars with highly polished floors and stylish young customers.

There are bars pounding with live music, smoke-filled cafés where young student radicals sit hunched over a warming beer.

For a country of this size, the number of beers Belgium produces is incredible. When you go into a bar you will probably be given a menu – not for food but for beer. There are white beers, blond beers, amber beers and dark beers, and others are flavoured with cherries or raspberries. Some are so light you feel you have drunk nothing more than a strong coffee. Others are extremely powerful.

Arenberg Galeries
Cinema

26 galerie de la Reine
Ⓜ Gare Centrale
☎ 512 80 63

Some bottles come wrapped in elaborate paper covers. Each one has a different glass, provided by the particular brewery. It is amazing how the bar staff remember which beer goes with which glass. Do sample a few, but do not rush them, and watch their strength. The rarer the beer,

Brussels after dark

the higher the price. In some bars you can buy a small plate of paté, smoked cheese, crackers and cold salad to soak up some of the alcohol.

Restaurants in L'Ilot Sacre

The nightclub scene is not as bold and prevalent as London, New York or Madrid but it is lively just the same. You will have no difficulty finding a venue that plays your kind of music. There are quite a number of jazz clubs, some of them well known on the European circuit. Other venues spin disco classics from the 1970s, and there is a plethora of modern dance clubs. Worth seeking out are the Latin American nightspots where you can dance salsa or merengue and then sit back, wipe the sweat from your brow, indulge in a margarita and watch the professionals at work on the dancefloor. Most clubs do not get going until around midnight and many stay buzzing until the sun breaks over the Brussels skyline.

Safety should be taken seriously, as in all big cities. Although Brussels is not known for high levels of street crime it pays to avoid walking alone at night draped in jewellery or cameras. The tourist office will be sure to point out any areas they feel deserve the "no-go" label. Beggars are a growing fact of life in Brussels, especially as more and more refugees from the Balkans arrive on the city's streets.

Brussels boasts a lively arts scene with scores of exhibitions and cultural events happening after dark. One of the main venues is the **Palais des Beaux Arts**

Théâtre de la Parc

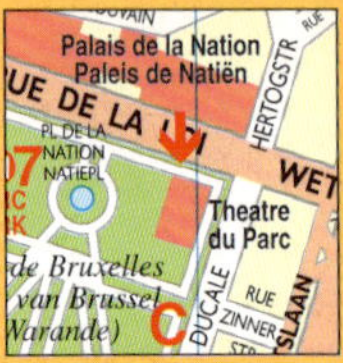

3 de la Loi
Ⓜ Arts-Loi
☎ 512 23 39

Galeries St. Hubert at night

(Centre of Fine Arts, page 19) on Rue Ravenstein. There visitors will find a concert hall, theatre, and exhibition space, as well as a cinema museum (**Musée du Cinéma**, page 20) with a screening room which still shows silent black and white movies.

Palais des Beaux-Arts

Rue Ravenstein
Ⓜ Gare Centrale
☎ 507 82 20

When you are in town there might also be something happening out at the **Parc des Expositions** in the Heysel district near the Atomium. This vast area was purpose built for conferences and grand events and exhibitions.

You could try your luck at the **Théâtre de la Monnaie** (Opera House). The seats are expensive and often sold out, but you might be lucky. You could turn up on the evening of a performance and see if any tickets have been returned. It is worth the effort to watch a performance in one of the world's leading opera houses.

Parc des Expositions

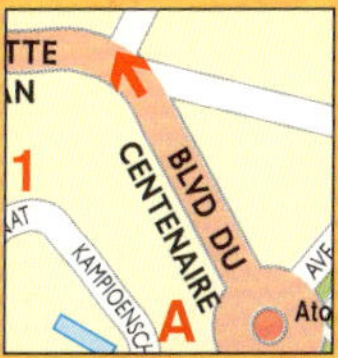

Heysel
Ⓜ Heysel

If you like your music heavier and louder head for **La Botanique** (page 17). This is now a top venue for rock bands.

Brussels has a fair share of cinemas and theatres showing contemporary films and plays, often in English with either French or Flemish subtitles.

For an evening with a difference head for the **Théâtre de Toone** (Puppet Theatre) and prepare to be amazed by the dexterity of the master puppeteers hiding in the wings.

Theatres

Théâtre National *(Centre Rogier, Place Rogier, Ⓜ Rogier, ☎ 203 53 03.)*

Beursschouwburg *(28 rue Auguste Orts, Ⓜ Bourse, ☎ 513 82 90.)*

Concert Halls

AB *(Boulevard Anspach 114, Ⓜ Bourse, ☎ 512 59 86.)*

Cirque Royal *(Rue de l'Enseignement 81, Ⓜ Madou, ☎ 218 20 15.)*

Rock Music

Magazin 4 *(Rue du Magasin 4, Ⓜ Yser, ☎ 223 34 74.)*

Jazz

Au Travers *(11 rue Traversiere, Ⓜ Botanique, ☎ 218 40 86.)*

Sounds *(28 rue de la Tulipe, Ⓜ Porte de Namur, ☎ 512 92 50.)*

Blues

Flanagan's *(55 boulevard de l'Empereur, Ⓜ Gare Centrale, ☎ 502 52 88.)*

Cinemas

Kinepolis *(20 boulevard du Centenaire, Ⓜ Heysel, ☎ 474 26 04.)*

Nightclubs

Mirano Continental *(38 chaussée de Louvain, Ⓜ Madou, ☎ 218 57 72.)*

La Botanique

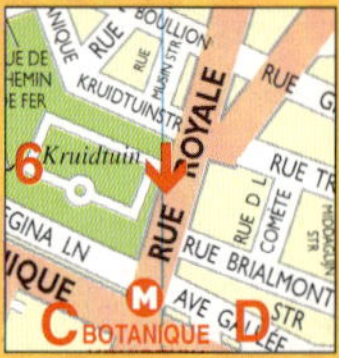

236 rue Royale
Ⓜ Botanique
☎ 226 12 11

Théâtre de Toone

6 impasse Schuddeveld, Petite rue des Bouchers
Ⓜ Bourse
☎ 511 7137

Brussels is lively at night

Visitor Information

CHILDREN

Brussels has several museums and attractions of interest to children. The **Musée des Bandes Dessinées** (page 15), the **Musée du Cinema** (page 20), **Mini Europe** (page 28), the **Atomium** (page 28) and, of course, the **Musée des Enfants** (page 35) are perennial favourites.

The **Théâtre de Toone** (page 56) stages puppet performances suitable for all the family.

CUSTOMS

Import restrictions for non-EU residents are: **Tobacco**: 200 cigarettes; **Alcohol**: 2 litres of wine plus 1 litres of spirits.

Import restrictions for EU residents are: **Tobacco**: 800 cigarettes; **Alcohol**: 90 litres of wine plus 10 litres of spirits.

ELECTRIC CURRENT

Electricity in Belgium runs on 220V with a two-pin plug.

HEALTH AND SAFETY

EU residents are entitled to emergency health services enjoyed by Belgians on the state system. As this does not cover all medical situations, both EU and non-EU nationals are advised to take out comprehensive travel insurance which includes medical coverage.

A wedding party in the Grand Place

Bargain hunting at a Brussels market

For the treatment of minor ailments, go to a pharmacy. These are recognisable by a green cross, and some are open 24 hours a day.

Pickpockets are rife in touristy and crowded areas such as the Grand Place, so take extra care of your belongings.

HOTELS

Below is a selection of hotels for various budgets in the centre of Brussels. 💰 = 2000BF for a standard double room per night.

Le Meridien *(3 Carrefour de l'Europe, Ⓜ Gare Centrale, ☎ 548 42 11.)* 💰 💰 💰 💰 💰

Hilton Brussels *(38 boulevard de Waterloo, Ⓜ Louise, ☎ 504 11 11.)* 💰 💰 💰 💰 💰

Stanhope Hotel *(9 rue du Commerce, Ⓜ Trone, ☎ 506 91 11.)* 💰 💰 💰 💰

Sheraton Brussels Hotel & Towers *(3 place Rogier, Ⓜ Rogier, ☎ 224 31 11.)* 💰 💰 💰 💰

Amigo *(1-3 rue de l'Amigo, Ⓜ Bourse, ☎ 547 47 4.)* 💰 💰 💰

Crowne Plaza *(3 rue Gineste, Ⓜ Rogier, ☎ 203 62 00.)* 💰 💰 💰

Astrid *(11 place du Samedi, Ⓜ Ste. Catherine, ☎ 219 31 19.)* 💰 💰 💰

Du Congrès *(40-44 rue du Congrès, Ⓜ Madou, ☎ 217 18 90.)* 💰 💰 💰

Alfa Sablon *(2-8 rue de la Paille, Ⓜ Gare*

EMERGENCIES

Dial ☎ 101 for the police, ☎ 100 for the fire service and ☎ 100 for an ambulance.

Eating al fresco

Centrale, ☎ *513 60 40.)* $$$

Rembrandt *(42 rue de la Concorde,* Ⓜ *Louise,* ☎ *512 71 39.)* $$

Aris *(78-80 rue du Marché-aux-Herbes,* Ⓜ *Bourse,* ☎ *514 43 00.)* $$

Les Bluets *(124 rue Berckmans,* Ⓜ *hotel des Monnaies,* ☎ *534 39 83.)* $

Fouquets *(6 rue de la Bourse,* Ⓜ *Bourse,* ☎ *512 00 20.)* $

New Galaxy *(7a rue du Progrés,* Ⓜ *Rogier,* ☎ *203 47 76.)* $

La Légende *(35 rue du Lombard,* Ⓜ *Bourse,* ☎ *512 82 90.)* $

LANGUAGE

The English language is widespread in Brussels, especially in the tourist trade and most hotels. The majority of Brussels residents speak French.

Hello	*Bonjour*
Goodbye	*Au revoir*
Yes / No	*Oui / Non*
Thank you	*Merci*
Please	*S'il vous plait*
Do you speak English?	*Parlez-vous anglais?*
Sorry / Excuse me	*Pardon / Excusez-moi*
I don't understand	*Je ne comprends pas*
Where is...	*Où est...*
How much is it?	*C'est combien?*
I would like...	*Je voudrais...*
Open	*Ouvert*
Closed	*Fermé*
Entrance	*Entrée*
Exit	*Sortie*

PACKING

Brussels has a temperate climate. Take heavy coats in the winter and a jumper for evenings, even in midsummer. Take something waterproof all year round.

LEFT LUGGAGE

Baggage can be deposited for a small charge at the Gare du Midi next to the Eurostar terminal, and at the airport.

LOST PROPERTY

Items lost on public transport in Brussels end up at the **lost property office** at Avenue de la Toison d'Or 15 *(☎ 515 2394)*. Other losses should be sought at the **municipal police station** *(Rue du Marché au Charbon, ☎ 517 9611)*.

MAIL / POST

Post offices open from 9am-4pm Monday to Friday, and the **central post office** *(48a Avenue Fosny)* is open 24 hours a day, every day. Post Restante letters can be sent to any major post office. Post boxes are red.

MONEY

The Belgian franc (BF) comes in denominations of 100, 200, 500, 1,000, 5,000 and 10,000BF notes, and coins of 1, 5, 20 and 50BF.

You can exchange money at banks, the railway station, exchange offices or at the main post office. International credit and debit cards can be used in bank machines.

Most large establishments in the centre of Brussels accept travellers' cheques,

A city taxi

although the exchange rate might be quite high. Credit cards are widely accepted.

OPENING HOURS

Banks - Standard opening hours are 9am to 4pm Monday to Friday. Some close for an hour at lunchtime.

Bars / Restaurants - Many restaurants open just 6 days a week, closing on Monday or Tuesday. Some close as early as 10pm, but there are plenty of bars and cafés which are open into the early hours.

Museums / Galleries - This guide lists individual opening times under each museum's entry.

Shops - Business hours are generally 10am-6pm Monday to Saturday, and all but the very tourist-orientated establishments are closed on Sundays.

SPECIAL TRAVELLERS

Disabled - Brussels has been slow to provide access and facilities for disabled people. The **STIB** (Société des Transports Intercommunaux de Bruxelles) has provided information in Braille at some metro stations, and also runs a minibus service *(☎ 515 23 65)*.

Elderly - Concessions are available with proof of age. Where specified in this guide, ***for less*** discounts are available on

TIPPING

Service is normally included in restaurant bills, although many people add an extra 5-10%. Rounding up fares in taxis is the norm.

A market stall

Hôtel de Ville

top of the normal senior discount.

Students - Concessions are available at many attractions and museums when acceptable ID, such as an ISIC card, is produced. Where specified in this guide, ***for less*** discounts are available on top of the normal student discount.

Gay - The **ILGA** (International Gay and Lesbian Association) have premises at Rue du Marché au Charbon 81 *(☎ 502 2471)* which incorporate a meeting place, café, and information resource. A useful listings magazine, *Tels-Quels*, is also produced here.

TELEPHONES

Public phones accept coins or telecards, which are available at post offices, news stands and supermarkets. Phones are also being adapted to accept credit cards.

TOURIST INFORMATION

The **main tourist office** (TIB) is in the Hotel de Ville in the Grand Place *(☎ 513 89 40)* and opens until about 7pm in high season.

TOURS

A few companies organise guided walking or bus tours around the city, with themes including art nouveau architecture, the comic book trail and tours of Jewish Brussels. Most have commentaries in various languages. Information about all tours can be found at the TIB office in

TELEPHONE CODES

The country code for Belgium is ☎ 32.

The code for Brussels is ☎ 02, which must be added when making calls from outside the city.

Tourist Information Centre

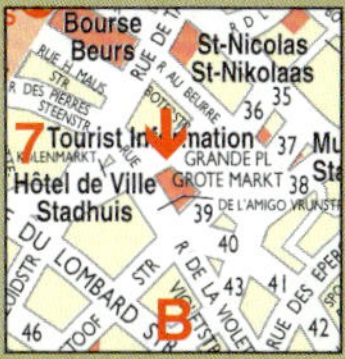

Grand Place
Ⓜ Gare Centrale
☎ 513 8940

Lacework, a Belgian speciality

the Grand Place.

TRANSPORT AROUND THE CITY

The **STIB** (Société des Transports Intercommunaux de Bruxelles) runs the city's trams, buses and metros, and the same tickets can be used on all three modes of transport. Public transport is extremely efficient.

Tickets can be purchased singly or, more economically, in strips of five or ten. A day-long travel card is even better value. You must stamp tickets yourself before embarking on your journey, or risk a hefty fine.

Route maps for all modes of transport are freely available from the tourist office.

Bus - Buses run by the STIB have two-digit numbers and link with trams to cover the whole city with about 30 lines. Tickets can be obtained from machines in metro stations or purchased when boarding. Some bus doors have to be opened manually.

Buses with longer numbers are run by the SNCV (Société Nationale des Chemins de Fer Vicinaux), a branch of the national railway service, and STIB tickets cannot be used on them.

TRANSPORT FROM THE AIRPORT

Brussels airport is about 12 km (8 miles) away at Zaventem. Trains depart for the Gare Centrale and Gare du Nord every 20 minutes from 6am to midnight. The journey takes 20 minutes. It is by far the best way to reach the city, as the bus service is infrequent.

Metro - The metro began operation in 1976 and is efficient and clean. There are three metro lines, and station entrances have a blue sign with a white M. Tickets must be purchased and stamped before you board.

Pre-metro - Trams become 'pre-metro' when they use metro lines underground, crossing the city north to south.

Trams - Trams are the more pleasant way to travel, although the overland ones are slower than pre-metro ones.

Taxis - Taxis are not hailed in the street. There are ranks outside railway stations and at major intersections, including the Bourse.

Walking - The city centre is small enough to cross on foot, but beware of traffic.

USEFUL TELEPHONE NUMBERS

Airport Information - ☎ *723 31 11 (24 hours).*

Central Police Station - ☎ *517 9870.*

Directory Enquiries (local) - ☎ *1307,* (international) - ☎ *1304.*

Emergency Dentist - ☎ *426 10 26.*

Emergency Doctor - ☎ *479 18 18.*

Railway Enquiries - ☎ *203 36 40.*

STIB Information - ☎ *515 2000.*

CREDITS

Principal photography:
A.F. Kersting, Photobank, Mecky Fögeling.

A Brussels tram

Index

Musée de la Ville de Bruxelles

2 admissions for the price of 1 at the **Musée de la Ville de Bruxelles** (page 11)

Valid from March 1, 1999

Musée du Costume et de la Dentelle

2 admissions for the price of 1 at the **Musée du Costume et de la Dentelle** (page 13)

Valid from March 1, 1999

Musée de Transport Urbain Bruxellois

2 admissions for the price of 1 at the **Musée de Transport Urbain Bruxellois** (page 35)

Valid from March 1, 1999

Musée David and Alice Van Buuren

2 admissions for the price of 1 at the **Musée David and Alice Van Buuren** (page 40)

Valid from March 1, 1999

Ce coupon donne droit aux réduction suivantes au **Musée de la Ville de Bruxelles** (page 11):

2 entrées pour le prix d'une: chaque entrée achetée vous donne droit á une entrée gratuite d'une valeur égale ou inférieure

Ce coupon donne droit aux réduction suivantes au **Musée du Costume et de la Dentelle** (page 13):

2 entrées pour le prix d'une: chaque entrée achetée vous donne droit á une entrée gratuite d'une valeur égale ou inférieure

Ce coupon donne droit aux réduction suivantes au **Musée de Transport Urbain Bruxellois** (page 35):

2 entrées pour le prix d'une: chaque entrée achetée vous donne droit á une entrée gratuite d'une valeur égale ou inférieure

Ce coupon donne droit aux réduction suivantes au **Musée David and Alice Van Buuren** (page 40):

2 entrées pour le prix d'une: chaque entrée achetée vous donne droit á une entrée gratuite d'une valeur égale ou inférieure

Musée Charlier

2 admissions for the price of 1 at the **Musée Charlier** (page 16)

Valid from March 1, 1999

Musée des Enfants

2 admissions for the price of 1 at the **Musée des Enfants** (page 35)

Valid from March 1, 1999

Musée du Cinéma

2 admissions for the price of 1 at the **Musée du Cinéma** (page 20)

Valid from March 1, 1999

Musée Erasmus

2 admissions for the price of 1 at the **Musée Erasmus** (page 41)

Valid from March 1, 1999

Ce coupon donne droit aux réduction suivantes au **Musée Charlier** (page 16):

2 entrées pour le prix d'une: chaque entrée achetée vous donne droit á une entrée gratuite d'une valeur égale ou inférieure

Ce coupon donne droit aux réduction suivantes au **Musée des Enfants** (page 35):

2 entrées pour le prix d'une: chaque entrée achetée vous donne droit á une entrée gratuite d'une valeur égale ou inférieure

Ce coupon donne droit aux réduction suivantes au **Musée du Cinéma** (page 20):

2 entrées pour le prix d'une: chaque entrée achetée vous donne droit á une entrée gratuite d'une valeur égale ou inférieure

Ce coupon donne droit aux réduction suivantes au **Musée Erasmus** (page 41):

2 entrées pour le prix d'une: chaque entrée achetée vous donne droit á une entrée gratuite d'une valeur égale ou inférieure

Cathédrale St. Michel et Ste. Gudule

2 admissions for the price of 1 at the **Cathédrale St. Michel et Ste. Gudule** (page 17)

Valid from March 1, 1999

Museum de l'Institut Royal des Sciences Naturelles

2 admissions for the price of 1 at the **Museum de l'Institut Royal des Sciences Naturelles** (page 31)

Valid from March 1, 1999

Customer Response Card

We would like to hear your comments about the ***Brussels for less Compact Guide*** so that we can improve it. Please complete the information below and mail this card. One card will be picked out at random to win a free holiday. No stamp is required, either in Belgium or your own country.

Name: ....

Address: ....

Tel. no.: ....

If you bought the book, where did you buy it from? ....

If you were given the book, which tour operator gave it to you? ....

Number of people travelling in your party ....

How many days were you in Brussels? ....

Did you like the guidebook? ....

What did you like about it? ....

....

Would you recommend it to a friend? ....

Would you be more interested in a tour operator's package if you knew it included the *Brussels for less Compact Guide*? ....

Any other comments ....

....

Ce coupon donne droit aux réduction suivantes à la **Cathédrale St. Michel et Ste. Gudule** (page 17):

2 entrées pour le prix d'une: chaque entrée achetée vous donne droit á une entrée gratuite d'une valeur égale ou inférieure

Ce coupon donne droit aux réduction suivantes au **Museum de l'Institut Royal des Sciences Naturelles** (page 30):

2 entrées pour le prix d'une: chaque entrée achetée vous donne droit á une entrée gratuite d'une valeur égale ou inférieure

By air mail
Par avion

NE PAS AFFRANCHIR
NO STAMP REQUIRED

IBRS/CCRI NUMBER: PHQ-D/2560/W

RESPONSE PAYEE
GRANDE-BRETAGNE

Metropolis International (UK) Limited
222 Kensal Road
LONDON, GREAT BRITAIN
W10 5BN